150
Acting Scenes

By
Vin Morreale, Jr.

Cover Design by Amanda Michelle Morreale

ISBN: 978-0-9991473-4-4

academyartspress.com

All Rights Reserved.
Copyright © 2018 by Vin Morreale, Jr.

Also by Vin Morreale, Jr.

ACADEMY ARTS PRESS
academyartspress.com/titles

300 Monologues

Knowing When To Leave
Dark Wilderness & Other Stories

Mabel The Maple

DRAMATIC PUBLISHING
dramaticpublishing.com/authors/profile/view/url/vin-morreale-jr

Breaking & Entering
Uncool
Nicky's Secret
Burning Up The Stage
The Happy Holidays Collection
Slight Indulgences
Southern Discomfort
House of The Seven Gables

ELDRIDGE PUBLISHING
histage.com/search?q=Morreale

The Fairyland Detective Agency
Sonoma White & The Seven Dolts
Fairies, Fantasies & Just Plain Fun

TABLE OF CONTENTS

About This Book	4
Acting Without Limits	6
Dramatic Scenes	9
Comedic Scenes	82

For permission to use any of these scenes in a performance or showcase, or to learn about our school discounts, email vin@academyarts.com.

Want to sharpen your acting skills, plus have a chance to showcase your talent to a national audience?

Visit 300monologues.com

About This Book

Within these pages you will find a diverse collection of original scenes designed for two actors. Each scene runs from thirty seconds to four minutes in length, and is designed specifically for you to play, to practice, to enjoy and to entertain others.

Like it's companion book, **300 MONOLOGUES**, these pieces were written for my ***Burning Up The Stage Acting Workshops***, which I have conducted in major cities across the United States over the past thirty years. In order to provide a unique experience for my students, I committed to writing at least two new monologues and one new scene for every workshop I conducted. At times I deeply regretted this personal challenge, especially on weeks when I was directing a play, casting a film, or working on one of my screenplays or novels. Yet, after a number of years, I found that I had created quite a collection of actor-centered exercises. And in 2018, I decided to share them with the rest of the acting community.

Together, **300 MONOLOGUES** and **150 ACTING SCENES** represent only a fraction of the original material my workshop students have had the opportunity to work on. Some were written to highlight a specific topic we were covering in a particular workshop, such as Personal Chemistry, Restrained Anger, Jealousy & Selflessness, Portraying Family Relationships, and so on. Others were devised to show how even farcical comedy can be far more effective, when the characters are played with sincerity and unflagging commitment.

For an often overlooked aspect of playing even a short piece is to realize that every word of dialogue is extremely important to your character at that exact moment in the scene. It should not be said simply because it is the next line in the script. It must be said because it is that character's way of engaging the other person in the scene, attempting to persuade him or her to give a very specific action, emotion or response. Every one of your fellow actor's lines is designed to accomplish the same thing.

Identifying 'the want' or objective behind each line will inform how you will deliver that dialogue and portray that scene.

In order to demonstrate to my students how crucial this specific want should be, I intentionally crafted a number of scenes that were intentionally non-specific in nature. Their meaning could be taken any number of different ways. This forced the actors to make clear choices as to who these characters are, what is happening in the scene, what the relationship between the two characters is, what each character hopes to gain or avoid, where the action is taking place, and why is it happening at that precise moment in time. Whenever a scene failed to work, it was often because the actors performing the scene had no clear idea, or held wildly different answers to those questions.

For example, a line simple as "What are you doing here?" takes on entirely different significance when it is uttered by someone discovering a thief in his living room in the middle of the night; an exhausted wife confronting the abusive husband she has thrown out weeks before; a frustrated boss bumping into an employee at a restaurant, after that employee had called in sick that morning; or a harried sibling, whose surprise party was ruined when the guest of honor arrives too early. In each of these cases, the line of dialogue will be laced with different emotions, intensity, and familiarity. Be bold, make choices and bring your own intuition to the piece.

I believe the best use of this book is to choose characters you feel are most unlike yourself, and scenes that do not necessarily play to your strengths. Most importantly, have fun with them. Take the same scene and play it a number of different ways, by changing your answers to the questions above.

The goal of this book is to expand your range as an actor. If you perform every scene over a number of months or years, you will build up your retinue of stock characters, and develop emotional muscles that will aid you in upcoming auditions and roles.

I wish you fun,

Vin Morreale, Jr.

Acting Without Limits

It is a natural human tendency to rely on our strengths, while avoiding those things we are less comfortable doing. Narrowing our efforts to only familiar choices keeps us safely within our comfort zone. Unfortunately, the more we narrow our focus, the less opportunity we have to grow beyond our current abilities.

As actors, we quickly discover the types of characters we are adept at portraying. We bask in the applause or critical feedback, and then go after similar roles with greater frequency. It's in our wheelhouse. It's what we do. The more roles we take on that resemble our chosen archetypes - such as sullen teen, passionate lawyer, anguished lover, or vicious criminal - the more we are typecast, or seen by others as only being able to play those specific characters. As a result, we miss out on so many more challenging opportunities.

The subtly seductive nature of positive reinforcement gradually transforms our comfort zone into an ever-tightening straitjacket. We even see this in some legendary actors, who as the decades fly by, seem to be playing increasingly strident variations of themselves in movie after movie. Great notoriety can often be a significant burden for a major star. Fortunately, there are those, such as Meryl Streep, who select roles as varied as her own impressive talents. And as such, she resists the siren song of self-characterization, choosing instead to continually reinvent herself with each new challenge.

That is why acting classes can be so valuable to actors at every stage of their development. Just as a champion golfer or professional baseball payer may quietly seek out the advice of a new coach, in order to uncover bad habits that may have crept into his swing, so to does a successful actor need to revisit an acting coach to recognize and eliminate any bad habits or too-easy characterizations he or she may lapse into without recognizing them as such.

The best acting classes encourage actors to expand well beyond their comfort zones, allowing them to dive deeply into roles and situations they may not otherwise have a chance to explore. The solid dramatic actor may find she excels at comedy. The facile comedian may take a stab at a period drama. Each may test their abilities with a more physically demanding role, while an actor with an overpowering physical presence may gain valuable insights by playing a shy, less expressive character. In this way, acting classes bring the 'play' back to the craft of acting. For the true beauty of children is that they have yet to place limits on their own imagination. That is why they can slip into and out of playful roles with relative ease. It is only as we grow older, that we internalize layer after layer of negative voices. Gradually allowing our inner critics to bend us into tighter and tighter definitions of ourselves.

 I have a difference of philosophy with those acting classes or coaches who practice tearing down or humiliating their students, as a way of helping them 'discover' their inner selves, or 'purify' their technique. Bullying in the name of art is still bullying, and instructors who need to enhance their reputation by beating down others may not always be worthy of the respect they demand.

 I believe any artist does his or her best work when they are free to try new things in a safe and supportive environment. Embracing the freedom to fail occasionally. This does not mean that all work should be equally praised; simply that new challenges and risky character choice are encouraged, so that all can explore the outer limits of their current abilities. This enables them to discover specific areas they need to work on, in order to become even more convincing in their craft.

 In order to grow, we must always be willing to risk. When the boundaries of our comfort zone become set in stone, we will never learn how much more we could have accomplished.

 Please use the many acting scenes in this book to try on a variety of new skins and delve into different characters. Risk having no preconceived notions of what you cannot do, but rather embrace the joy of the limitless soul. Become open and childlike, and never forget the exhiliration of simply playing a part outside of your self-imposed boundaries.

Dramatic Scenes

1.

FIRST ACTOR: What are you doing?

SECOND ACTOR: Making breakfast for your father. You know how cranky he gets when he doesn't get his French toast on Sunday mornings.

FIRST ACTOR: Mom, it's Thursday.

SECOND ACTOR: Already? Well, that explains why he's been cranky all week.

FIRST ACTOR: It's Thursday, and it's after midnight.

SECOND ACTOR: I know that. You don't think I know that? It's Thursday. Thursday. And I was…you know…um, teasing you.

FIRST ACTOR: Mom…

SECOND ACTOR: It's okay. I just felt the need to cook something.

FIRST ACTOR: If that's all…

SECOND ACTOR: It's just that some nights I can't sleep. The hospital bills. My migraines. The worries about your father's health. He moans in his sleep, do you know that? It's an awful sound. Shakes me right out of my dreams. Some nights it all seems like it's too much. But it makes me happy to pamper him now and then. Is that so bad?

FIRST ACTOR: Mom…

SECOND ACTOR: Why is that a bad thing?

FIRST ACTOR: Mom…Dad's gone. Six years now. And he always hated your French toast.

SECOND ACTOR: I know that too… You don't think I know that?

FIRST ACTOR: Come back to bed, Mom. It's late.

SECOND ACTOR: It is late, isn't it?

FIRST ACTOR: Come on. Let's get you something for that headache….

2.

FIRST ACTOR: Is it cold in here, or is it me?

SECOND ACTOR: It's you.

FIRST ACTOR: I don't mean the temperature. I mean the way everyone is treating me.

SECOND ACTOR: Like I said, it's you.

FIRST ACTOR: What's that supposed to mean?

SECOND ACTOR: They're good people. You could try being a little nicer to them. Y'know, friendlier?

FIRST ACTOR: I am being friendly! I even said hi to Roy and Eleanor. And had to stand there and listen while they went on and on about that new baby of theirs... Give me a break. Like they were the first people on earth to ever squirt out a kid ...

SECOND ACTOR: Roy and Eleanor have been trying for five years. You could pretend you cared for five minutes.

FIRST ACTOR: Oh, so it's all my fault?

SECOND ACTOR: It's not about fault. It's about fun. These are people I grew up with. People I've known all my life. You act like you're doing all of us a big favor just by being here.

FIRST ACTOR: Oh, that's just great! I drag myself to this stupid party, and put up with your stupid friends and their stupid attitudes... and somehow, I get the blame?

SECOND ACTOR: No. You're right. You're absolutely right. It's not your fault. It's everybody else's... Look, I'm going to go back in and talk to my stupid friends for a while. Why don't you just wait out here. Okay?

FIRST ACTOR: Okay. *(Pause, then...)* You're not coming back, are you?

SECOND ACTOR: *(Smiles)* I don't know. It's kind of cold out here. *(Exits)*

3.

FIRST ACTOR: I'm sorry. I said I'm sorry.

SECOND ACTOR: I heard you.

FIRST ACTOR: So, we're good, right?

SECOND ACTOR: Seriously? You think any of this even closely resembles good?

FIRST ACTOR: Cut the attitude. You know how I hate that.

SECOND ACTOR: Or what? You going to hit me again? Choke me like the last time? Maybe break a finger or something because I finally have the nerve to say enough?

FIRST ACTOR: You got a mouth on you, you know that?

SECOND ACTOR: Yeah. You bloodied it enough over the years.

FIRST ACTOR: You know I got a temper. You don't like it, don't go pissing me off with that mouth of yours. That's all.

SECOND ACTOR: Right. It's my fault. You had me believing that for a long time. But now you gotta smack the kids around. Scare them to death, so they run and hide in their room every time they know Daddy's been out drinking.

FIRST ACTOR: I work hard. If I want a drink now and then, that's my business.

SECOND ACTOR: No. Those kids are your business! You're teaching your seven year-old son that a real man gets flat-out drunk and uses his fist on a woman anytime he feels like it. And you're teaching Emily she can expect more of the same when she grows up.

FIRST ACTOR: Those kids love me. You can't say they don't!

SECOND ACTOR: Of course, they love you! That's the saddest part of all. They love you so much, it makes them swallow your excuses every time you say Mom had it coming, or you promise never to do it again.

FIRST ACTOR: I won't...

SECOND ACTOR: It makes them pretend they don't see the bruises and black eyes. Or hear all the screaming and swearing. And it makes them blame the police for arresting you, every time you beat up the neighbors for having the nerve to park their cars anywhere near our house.

FIRST ACTOR: I've got good kids. They stick up for their dad!

SECOND ACTOR: Yes, they do. Even when he continually beats them down, physically or emotionally. You know, they begged me not to call the police the last time you busted my lip? They were in tears, knowing you were only one more complaint away from doing serious time. My own children would rather I shut up and take your beatings, then let you take responsibility for being a serial abuser. My own children...

FIRST ACTOR: I already said I got a temper! I already said I was sorry! What the hell more do you want me to say?!

SECOND ACTOR: Say goodbye. To me and the kids. At least until you learn to be a real man. Or at least act like one.

FIRST ACTOR: Goodbye? Oh, so you think you're leavin' me, huh?

SECOND ACTOR: Just for a while. Until you get your drinking under control.

FIRST ACTOR: I got my drinking under control. But you and your mouth sure as hell don't make it easy.

SECOND ACTOR: Then let me make it easy for you... Me and the kids are moving in with my mother.

FIRST ACTOR: Yeah? And what makes you think I'm gonna let any of you go?

4.

FIRST ACTOR: Who are you?

SECOND ACTOR: You don't remember me?

FIRST ACTOR: No. I never saw you before in my life.

SECOND ACTOR: C'mon. Tell the truth.

FIRST ACTOR: Get away from me! I don't know you.

SECOND ACTOR: Sweetheart, please…calm down…

FIRST ACTOR: I'm not your sweetheart! Get away from me! I don't know you! I've never seen you before in. my life!

SECOND ACTOR: So that's how it's gonna be, huh?

FIRST ACTOR: Just go. Just leave me alone. Please.

SECOND ACTOR: If that's the way you want it. *(Exits)*

FIRST ACTOR: *(Softly. After he leaves)* Goodbye, Richard…

5.

FIRST ACTOR: I heard them outside. They're coming.

SECOND ACTOR: I know. I heard them too. But hey, all good things come to an end… Milk spoils. Pets die. People drift apart… The universe hurtles toward entropy…

FIRST ACTOR: You are so strange.

SECOND ACTOR: Yup.

FIRST ACTOR: What are you going to tell them?

SECOND ACTOR: I dunno. Anything but what they really want to know, I guess. You can count on me.

FIRST ACTOR: Can I?

SECOND ACTOR: Hard to say. Ultimately, you can't really count on anything… Milk spoils. Pets die. People drift apart… The universe hurtles toward entropy…

6.

FIRST ACTOR: Excuse me. Can you tell me where I can find…?

SECOND ACTOR: *(Without looking up)* Four blocks down on the left. Second door. Ask for Billy.

FIRST ACTOR: But I didn't even tell you what I was looking for?

SECOND ACTOR: You don't have to. It's four blocks down on the left. Second door. Ask for Billy.

FIRST ACTOR: What if all I wanted was to find a bathroom?

SECOND ACTOR: They have one there, too.

FIRST ACTOR: And what if…?

SECOND ACTOR: Look… I been livin' here ten, eleven years now. I seen 'em all. Fans, groupies, paparazzi, movie producers, stalkers and wannabees… There's only one reason people come to this side of town…and that reason is four blocks down on the left.

FIRST ACTOR: I find your attitude highly offensive. You don't even consider the possibility that I might be different. That maybe I'm here to…

SECOND ACTOR: *(Finally looking up, and not pleasantly)* Here to…what?

FIRST ACTOR: Here to…well… *(withers under Second Actor's glare)* …You, um…said four blocks down on the left?

SECOND ACTOR: Second door. Ask for Billy.

FIRST ACTOR: Uh… thank you. I'll be um, going now… *(Embarrassed)* Thanks again… *(Exits)*

SECOND ACTOR: *(Grumbles)* … I hate this place…

7.

FIRST ACTOR: We need to talk.

SECOND ACTOR: Uh oh. That's never a good sign. Can't it wait until after this commercial? I'm a big fan of dancing farm animals.

FIRST ACTOR: I'm serious.

SECOND ACTOR: I know. That's why I'm being evasive.

FIRST ACTOR: You've been sleeping on my couch for five months now…

SECOND ACTOR: It's been that long? Seems like only yesterday.

FIRST ACTOR: No, yesterday you threw up on my floor. Last week you told the landlady she looked like she got a face transplant from a baboon. And the week before that you tied the cat to the ceiling fan.

SECOND ACTOR: Yeah. Good times.

FIRST ACTOR: No. They were not good times. Just the same messes I've had to cover for you ever since we were kids.

SECOND ACTOR: No one said you have to cover anything for me. I can take care of myself.

FIRST ACTOR: Yeah? Then why are you sleeping on my couch? Why haven't you ever been able to hold even the simplest job for more than three weeks?

SECOND ACTOR: I can't help it if the people I worked for were all a bunch of…

FIRST ACTOR: It's not the people you worked for. *(Cutting him off)* Every single one of them knew you had a problem. If not when they hired you, they learned pretty quickly after that. I know you have a problem. The only one who doesn't know you have a problem is you. Or at least you don't admit it.

SECOND ACTOR: So…what? You gonna lecture me now? Set me straight? Let me know what a worthless piece of crap brother I am? Because I gotta tell ya, sis. You can't make me feel any more worthless than I do already, I guarantee you that. *(Turns back to the TV)* Man, I love this one! Who comes up with these commercials anyway?

FIRST ACTOR: I think it is time for you to go.

SECOND ACTOR: What? You're kicking me out?

FIRST ACTOR: For your own good.

SECOND ACTOR: Ha! That's just what Mom and Dad said. Right before they threw me out on the street. Out on the street, with nothing but thirteen bucks in my pocket.

FIRST ACTOR: Thirteen bucks? On top of all the wedding silver and Mom's jewelry you stole! You know what it did to Dad to have to take the bus all the way down to that seedy pawn shop to buy back all of Mom's jewelry?

SECOND ACTOR: Hey, you think whatever you want, or use whatever kind of excuse, you think you need to, to let yourself feel better about kicking me to the curb.

FIRST ACTOR: I'm not kicking you to the curb. There's a rehab clinic out on Sixth Street. I already booked a room for you. They can help…

SECOND ACTOR: I don't need rehab, and I don't need your guilt trip! Got it?! I'm outta here. *(Grabbing clothes)* See ya around. sis. Sorry about peeing on the couch. *(Exits angrily)*

FIRST ACTOR: *(Softly)* That's what families are for…

8.

FIRST ACTOR: Nobody can ever love me… Nobody should ever love me…

SECOND ACTOR: How can you say that?

FIRST ACTOR: Because of who I am. Because of what I'd do, if I had a chance. If I knew I could get away with it. They fall for the show, but they get hurt by the reality. And the reality is…I'm not worth the pain I cause…

SECOND ACTOR: It's amazing how you can turn self-loathing into self-pity…and then use that as a cry for affection.

FIRST ACTOR: Pretty messed up, huh?

SECOND ACTOR: Yeah. It's what I love about you.

9.

FIRST ACTOR: I'm worried about you.

SECOND ACTOR: You should be.

FIRST ACTOR: Is that some kind of threat? Are you threatening me?

SECOND ACTOR: Maybe. Maybe not. It's hard to tell anymore.

FIRST ACTOR: You're screwed up, you know that?

SECOND ACTOR: Look. You've done your part. You've expressed your concern. You've made your judgments. You've covered your butt. I don't see that we have anything left to talk about.

FIRST ACTOR: Okay. If that's the way you want it. Just don't do anything stupid, okay?

SECOND ACTOR: Too late for that.

10.

FIRST ACTOR: What are you doing here? *(No reply)* What are you doing here?! *(Still no answer)* Did you hear me?! What are you doing here?!

SECOND ACTOR: *(Softly)* Where else did you expect me to go?

FIRST ACTOR: Anywhere. Everywhere. Drop off the end of the earth. Crawl down the garbage disposal. I don't care. It really doesn't matter to me where you go.

SECOND ACTOR: She's dead, you know.

FIRST ACTOR: What?

SECOND ACTOR: Died in her sleep. Natural causes. At least, that's the official story. But we both know the truth, don't we?

FIRST ACTOR: I don't know what you're talking about.

SECOND ACTOR: Sure, you do. Because the unofficial story... The real version...is that she screamed for hours...in more pain than a normal person could ever imagine.

FIRST ACTOR: I don't need to hear this.

SECOND ACTOR: Yes, you do. Because all that time she was suffering...through all the agony and the whimpers and tears... she was screaming out one name. Yours. Over and over and over again.

FIRST ACTOR: I'm sorry to hear it. I really am. But what are you doing here?

SECOND ACTOR: Keeping a promise.

FIRST ACTOR: What promise.

SECOND ACTOR: The one I made to her right before she died. *(Pulls out a gun)* Now ask me again what I'm doing here...

11.

FIRST ACTOR: *(Stunned)* Wow...

SECOND ACTOR: I'm so sorry...

FIRST ACTOR: So, this is what it feels like? Having your heart stepped on and...and ground into the dust...

SECOND ACTOR: I meant to tell you. I really tried.

FIRST ACTOR: Kinda sucks, doesn't it?

SECOND ACTOR: It's New York. Like I've always dreamed of. An opportunity of a lifetime for me.

FIRST ACTOR: ...wow... just wow...

SECOND ACTOR: It doesn't have to be the end. In fact, it could actually be a good thing for us.

FIRST ACTOR: You think so?

SECOND ACTOR: You said you needed a change. And you would really like it in New York. It's a real artist's town. They'd love you there.

FIRST ACTOR: Oh? So, you're doing this for me, huh?

SECOND ACTOR: No, but Jack makes a lot of money. I could set you up. You'd never have to work at those pissy part-time jobs again. You could go to auditions all day. I could get you in one of those trendy downtown lofts overlooking the theatre district...

FIRST ACTOR: As what? Your male mistress? The guy you escape to every other Thursday? Or when things get boring at home with...what's his name? Jack?

SECOND ACTOR: I meant to tell you about him...

FIRST ACTOR: You should have. Finding it out from your kids really kicked the wind outa me, you know? In fact, finding out you had kids was a bit of a shock, too.

SECOND ACTOR: Look, I'm so sorry.

FIRST ACTOR: Yeah. So…when do you leave?
SECOND ACTOR: Not for another month or so.
FIRST ACTOR: Are you serious?
SECOND ACTOR: I meant to tell you. I really did.
FIRST ACTOR: Yeah…

12.

FIRST ACTOR: Well…did you like the movie?
SECOND ACTOR: That piece of pedantic crap? It was so poor, it could qualify for food stamps. The characters were one-dimensional. And I haven't heard that many clichés since the last presidential debate.
FIRST ACTOR: Actually, I kind of enjoyed it.
SECOND ACTOR: How can you say that? It was sappy, derivative and completely ridiculous. The only award it could hope to win is 'Best Waste of Time.'
FIRST ACTOR: I thought it was fun.
SECOND ACTOR: Come on. You can't possibly be that shallow.
FIRST ACTOR: Sure, I can. I am attracted to you, despite your rude and abrasive personality. Your constant condescension. And speaking of clichés, you only hate that movie because you read an online review telling you to hate it. And you love to pass off other people's ideas as your own.
SECOND ACTOR: I do not!
FIRST ACTOR: Admit it. If it wasn't for Twitter and a few obscure and pretentious podcasts, you would have nothing at all to say to anyone.
SECOND ACTOR: This date isn't working out too well, is it?
FIRST ACTOR: Let's just say, I don't see a third act for us.

13.

FIRST ACTOR: *(Handing over a check)* That's it. Payment in full. We're done here.

SECOND ACTOR: Wait a minute… this is less than half of what we agreed on?

FIRST ACTOR: I know. But I figure it's the absolute minimum you'll take now.

SECOND ACTOR: But…but we had a deal?

FIRST ACTOR: That was then. This is now. Can't live in the past, you know.

SECOND ACTOR: Why are you doing this?

FIRST ACTOR: One…because I can. Two…because your desperate, and your desperation gives me greater leverage…which leads us back to one…because I can. So, you can either take the check, or take the chance you'll get a better offer before the bank repos your house. *(Long pause)* I'm waiting…

SECOND ACTOR: *(Pockets the check)* I hate you.

FIRST ACTOR: Of course, you do. Now get the hell off my property before I call the police.

14.

FIRST ACTOR: Why are you acting this way?

SECOND ACTOR: What way?

FIRST ACTOR: I don't know. Different. Not yourself.

SECOND ACTOR: Is that a bad thing?

FIRST ACTOR: Yeah. It's just not like you at all.

SECOND ACTOR: Maybe I got tired of being me. Or what everybody else told me I was supposed to be.

FIRST ACTOR: Oh, so now you're the big rebel? Like you're so much better than your friends?

SECOND ACTOR:	Not better. Just different. *(Pause)* I always felt all this pressure to fit in, y'know? To do what everybody expected me to do. To be like everyone else.
FIRST ACTOR:	That's life. Get used to it.
SECOND ACTOR:	But it's not my life. It's someone else's. Someone I don't want to be.
FIRST ACTOR:	What are you saying?
SECOND ACTOR:	I just suddenly realized…I have nothing in common with you. Any of you. Nothing at all.
FIRST ACTOR:	So that's the way it's gonna be, huh?
SECOND ACTOR:	*(Smiling. Walking off)* I think so…

15.

FIRST ACTOR:	Is this true? What you wrote?
SECOND ACTOR:	What do you care?
FIRST ACTOR:	What do you mean, 'what do I care?' This is terrible. It makes us both look bad.
SECOND ACTOR:	We are bad. We're disgusting. I'm tired of hiding behind all the lies and whispers, that's all.
FIRST ACTOR:	You don't know what you've done here.
SECOND ACTOR:	I know exactly what I've done. I've shown the world who we are. Who you are. What you're capable of. What you've always been capable of.
FIRST ACTOR:	Based on what? I never did half of the things you wrote here! I could never do anything like that.
SECOND ACTOR:	It doesn't matter. By the time this hits the Internet, ten or twenty million people will believe you could.
FIRST ACTOR:	I'll kill you for this.
SECOND ACTOR:	Then everything I wrote about you will come true. Rather ironic, isn't it?

16.

FIRST ACTOR: You wanted to see me?

SECOND ACTOR: Yes, Natalie. Please sit down. Tell me…are you happy here?

FIRST ACTOR: You're kidding, right?

SECOND ACTOR: Excuse me?

FIRST ACTOR: I've been one of the hardest working employees you ever had. I put in overtime almost every week. The quality of my work is the highest in this department.

SECOND ACTOR: All that has been noted in your annual reviews.

FIRST ACTOR: How kind of you. But I bet there's nothing in my file about how I have covered for your mistakes all these years. Or anything about me making you look even close to competent, which is really the hardest part of my job.

SECOND ACTOR: I'm detecting a bit of hostility here, Natalie.

FIRST ACTOR: Really? Too bad you didn't detect it after you passed me over for a raise six years in a row. Or when you promoted your nephew Benjamin over me. Even though he's only been working here four months and has the IQ of a brain-damaged lemur.

SECOND ACTOR: You'll be happy to know Benjamin was let go this morning. It seems he alienated our biggest client with some…um, inappropriate social media comments and photos.

FIRST ACTOR: I know. That's the reason they decided to take their entire account in-house, and then hire me to run the department. It seems they are making me a Vice President at nearly twice the salary I make here. So, you can consider this my exit interview, as well as my two-minute notice. *(Standing)* Have a nice day!

17.

FIRST ACTOR: Here it is. *(Handing her a note)*

SECOND ACTOR: What's that?

FIRST ACTOR: The number of the place that does my hair.

SECOND ACTOR: Why would I want that? Your hair always looks like roadkill.

FIRST ACTOR: You asked me to go look it up for you? You always said you liked my hair...

SECOND ACTOR: Oh, you believed that? That's really funny.

FIRST ACTOR: What do you mean?

SECOND ACTOR: I didn't want the number. I just wanted you gone. I needed some alone time with Chuck. Luckily, you were too dumb to pick up on that.

FIRST ACTOR: You were hitting on my boyfriend?

SECOND ACTOR: Wake up, girlfriend! He's hot. And he can do so much better than you. He can do me, for instance.

FIRST ACTOR: How could you? I thought you were my friend...

SECOND ACTOR: Again. Another thing you were too dumb to pick up on.

FIRST ACTOR: What do you mean?

SECOND ACTOR: *(Pulls out a different note)* It was his number I wanted. Not your lame hair stylist's.

FIRST ACTOR: He gave you his number?

SECOND ACTOR: And a hug, a long passionate kiss... Oh, and he's driving me home tonight, so you're going to need another ride. *(Happily)* Later!

18.

FIRST ACTOR: Guess what!

SECOND ACTOR: You're getting married.

FIRST ACTOR: What? Who told you?

SECOND ACTOR: Nobody told me. Nobody had to.

FIRST ACTOR: Then how did you know?

SECOND ACTOR: That silly grin on your face. That thrilled-to-death, semi-terrified, what-am-I-getting-myself-into look that says your life is about to change and you're not quite sure if you are ready for it.

FIRST ACTOR: It shows, huh?

SECOND ACTOR: Subtlety was never your strong suit. Who is it this time?

FIRST ACTOR: What do you mean, 'this time?'

SECOND ACTOR: Do I have to mention 2012? 2015? The two different engagements in 2017. And don't forget that head-over-heels romance last May?

FIRST ACTOR: Okay. Okay! I fall in love easily. Is that my fault?

SECOND ACTOR: Depends on your perspective. What do you say we ask 2012, 2015, the two in 2017, and…?

FIRST ACTOR: I don't know why I tell you anything. Can't you just be happy for me?

SECOND ACTOR: Of course, I'm happy for you. I'm always happy for you. The only one happier than me is the jewelry store that your love life is single handedly keeping in business.

FIRST ACTOR: You think I'm making another mistake?

SECOND ACTOR: Don't ask me that. Ask me to throw you a party. Ask me to help you pick out wedding invitations. But please don't ask me if you are making a mistake…

FIRST ACTOR: Why?

SECOND ACTOR:	Because then I'd have to tell you the truth…and we don't want to start all that again.
FIRST ACTOR:	You don't have to be like that.
SECOND ACTOR:	I'm trying not to be.
FIRST ACTOR:	Look. You know how I feel…
SECOND ACTOR:	I know. It's okay. I was 2012, and that was a long time ago. A very long time ago… So, you go get married and live happily ever after. And I'll just…I don't know…go on living, I guess.
FIRST ACTOR:	I love you, you know.
SECOND ACTOR:	I know. *(Smiles sadly)* But I have to go now… Congratulations, by the way. *(Exits)*

19.

FIRST ACTOR:	Is that everything?
SECOND ACTOR:	Yeah. I'm all packed, and the cab will be here any minute.
FIRST ACTOR:	Are you sure you want to go through with this?
SECOND ACTOR:	Do we have any choice?
FIRST ACTOR:	Yes! We can make this work. I can change. I promise you, I can change!
SECOND ACTOR:	Not enough. We both know that.
FIRST ACTOR:	Please don't go… Please.
SECOND ACTOR:	The saddest thing is…I left years ago. You just didn't notice until now.

20.

FIRST ACTOR: *(Tied to a chair)* Why…why are you doing this…?

SECOND ACTOR: It's funny. That's the first question they always ask. Like knowing why is going to make this whole thing easier for them. Trust me. It's not.

FIRST ACTOR: Please…I…I have a family.

SECOND ACTOR: That's the other thing they always say. Every time. Just like clockwork. 'Why are you doing this?' 'Please. I have a family.' As if somehow that's going to make a difference… But let me let you in on a little secret… Everybody has a family. Everybody is somebody's mother or father, son or daughter, brother or sister… or third cousin, twice removed. It don't make a damn bit of difference. You're still gonna die.

FIRST ACTOR: But…why.? Why?

SECOND ACTOR: Still need to know, huh? Still think that'll make you feel better?

FIRST ACTOR: …yes…

SECOND ACTOR: I could give you plenty of reasons. You screwed up. You made the wrong person angry. I'm getting paid a lot of money. *(Leans in & whispers)* But you want to know the real reason?

FIRST ACTOR: …yes…

SECOND ACTOR: Say please again.

FIRST ACTOR: …what?

SECOND ACTOR: Say it.

FIRST ACTOR: …please…

SECOND ACTOR: The real reason is…I enjoy this. I really do. Some people like to camp, or sail or watch football. I like to squeeze the life out of another human being. *(Picks up a knife)* Sucks for you, huh?

21.

FIRST ACTOR: Oh, you're home!

SECOND ACTOR: Yeah, surprise! I'm home. Where is he?

FIRST ACTOR: Where is who?

SECOND ACTOR: Don't play cute with me. You know who I'm talking about. Where is he?

FIRST ACTOR: What makes you think I know?

SECOND ACTOR: Because whenever something dirty is going down, you're right there in the middle of it. Whenever something involves any amount of lying, cheating, or a complete disregard for human emotions, you're the first person I thinks of.

FIRST ACTOR: Gee...and I thought you were just starting to like me.

SECOND ACTOR: I am. That's why I mentioned your good points first. If I didn't like you, I'd have repeated what I heard at Nick's the other night. Y'know, when you...

FIRST ACTOR: *(Quickly)* You shouldn't believe everything you hear.

SECOND ACTOR: Especially when it comes out of your mouth. Now, where is he?

FIRST ACTOR: He's...he's gone.

SECOND ACTOR: Gone? Like gone away? Like no longer a part of your life? Or gone, like dead?

FIRST ACTOR: Does it matter? He's gone. It's over.

SECOND ACTOR: Over?

FIRST ACTOR: Yeah. *(Softly)* You won.

SECOND ACTOR: Now that's the first thing I've ever heard you say that made sense.

22.

FIRST ACTOR: Still working on that song?

SECOND ACTOR: Uh huh.

FIRST ACTOR: How's it going?

SECOND ACTOR: Fine. I need to concentrate.

FIRST ACTOR: You need me to go away?

SECOND ACTOR: Not go away. Just…go away for now.

FIRST ACTOR: *(Sits)* I do that, you know. Every day and half the night. I go away. Tip toe through this apartment like a ghost, so I don't disturb your 'creative process.'

SECOND ACTOR: Can we talk about this later?

FIRST ACTOR: No. Because later never comes. Later is always 'after I get this verse,' or 'after I fix this messed up chord progression,' or 'after I unblock whatever creative constipation is keeping everyone from recognizing how friggin' brilliant I am!'

SECOND ACTOR: I don't need this right now.

FIRST ACTOR: You mean, what you don't need right now is me.

SECOND ACTOR: What is it you want from me, huh? I'm working here. Working hard, trying to kickstart this career. Trying to make this more than just some side gig or hobby. Make it something that'll bring in serious money. For you and for me.

FIRST ACTOR: Be honest. It's not about the money. It never was.

SECOND ACTOR: Okay. Maybe it's not. Maybe it's this obsession I have. Or fear. Or a crazy need to prove something to the world. Prove something to myself.

FIRST ACTOR: Prove what?

SECOND ACTOR: That I can be somebody! That I can really be somebody.

FIRST ACTOR:	But you are somebody. Whether you hit it big, or you never do more than play that guitar at our kitchen table. Either way. You will always be somebody to me.
SECOND ACTOR:	Maybe. But that somebody is not enough. I don't know why, but it isn't.
FIRST ACTOR:	I guess that's the difference between you and me. You want fame. Hunger for it. You need to be loved and admired by millions of screaming fans. You don't want the art, just the acclaim. That's your idea of being somebody.
SECOND ACTOR:	Every artist feels that. It's what keeps us going. Keeps us creating. Why is that so bad?
FIRST ACTOR:	It isn't. It's just that, I want to be somebody, too. What I want…all I ever wanted…was to be somebody *to you*. But that's not enough, is it? I'm not enough.
SECOND ACTOR:	Listen…
FIRST ACTOR:	It's okay. *(walking away)* Get back to work. And that chord progression sucks.

23.

FIRST ACTOR:	I can't make it.
SECOND ACTOR:	That's not my problem.
FIRST ACTOR:	Really. I'm done here. I got nothin' left.
SECOND ACTOR:	That's too bad.
FIRST ACTOR:	You can't leave me like this… I'll die. I'll just die right here. Do you want that on your conscience? Me on the ground. Knowing you didn't lift a finger to help me?
SECOND ACTOR:	Like I said. Not my problem. *(Exits)*

24.

FIRST ACTOR: You're home.

SECOND ACTOR: Yeah.

FIRST ACTOR: Where have you been?

SECOND ACTOR: Out.

FIRST ACTOR: I know that. I want to know where.

SECOND ACTOR: I've been out. That's all.

FIRST ACTOR: Out is a very big place. Out is getting in trouble with those loser friends you hang out with. Out is skipping out on your responsibilities and drinking yourself into oblivion. Out is everywhere you are not supposed to be.

SECOND ACTOR: It's not...

FIRST ACTOR: Out is squandering the last of our rent money on some get-rich sucker bet, that never seems to work out for you. Out is looking at someone else with eyes and thoughts that aren't meant for them, only for me. So, I'm asking you again. Where have you been?

SECOND ACTOR: Out.

FIRST ACTOR: That's all you've got to say? Out?

SECOND ACTOR: Okay, you really want to know? I've been out. Out working a second job, so I could by you something nice for our anniversary. So, I could buy you this.

(Throws a small box on the floor. First Actor opens it.)

FIRST ACTOR: *(Stunned)* I...I don't know what to say...

SECOND ACTOR: Don't say anything. *(Exiting)* I'm going out.

25.

FIRST ACTOR: We shouldn't be doing this.

SECOND ACTOR: I know.

FIRST ACTOR: It's not right. You know that, don't you? You understand how bad this is?

SECOND ACTOR: Yeah, I know. So let's just get it done, and done fast, okay?

FIRST ACTOR: And then what?

SECOND ACTOR: And then it's done. It's over. We move on.

FIRST ACTOR: And you can live with that?

SECOND ACTOR: Sure. Best not to think about it. Compartmentalize.

FIRST ACTOR: Compartmentalize?

SECOND ACTOR: Shove it way down deep. Bury it in a part of you that you don't ever intend to visit again. After that, you do your day-to-day. Get on with your life. Simple as that.

FIRST ACTOR: I'm not sure I can do that.

SECOND ACTOR: Well, you damn well should have thought of that before. Only now, you're committed. A hundred percent. You back out now and…

FIRST ACTOR: And what?

SECOND ACTOR: Do I have to spell it out for you? Huh? Do I?

FIRST ACTOR: No…

SECOND ACTOR: So…you ready to do this? I said, are you ready to do this?

FIRST ACTOR: I guess. *(Pause)* Compartmentalize?

SECOND ACTOR: Compartmentalize. Then get on with your life.

FIRST ACTOR: And that's all there is to it?

SECOND ACTOR: Trust me.

26.

FIRST ACTOR: I got the job.

SECOND ACTOR: Uh huh.

FIRST ACTOR: Did you hear me? I got the job!

SECOND ACTOR: *(Not looking up)* I heard you.

FIRST ACTOR: Well, aren't you going to congratulate me? I mean, this is huge. Huge!

SECOND ACTOR: *(Flatly)* Congratulations.

FIRST ACTOR: Okay, what is it?

SECOND ACTOR: What's what?

FIRST ACTOR: You. The attitude.

SECOND ACTOR: Nothing. I'm tired. That's all.

FIRST ACTOR: No. It's more than that. There's something else. A hostility or something.

SECOND ACTOR: I'm tired. That's all.

FIRST ACTOR: What is it? You can't take change? Are you committed to squalor? Afraid of finally having money? Afraid of success? *(Slow realization)* Or…are you just afraid of *my* success.

SECOND ACTOR: Right.

FIRST ACTOR: That's it, isn't it? You're jealous! You're jealous that someone finally recognized how good I am. What I have to offer. Admit it! You're jealous because this is about me, and not you, for once!

SECOND ACTOR: It's always about you! Every stupid dream. Every shattered hope. If I'm jealous, it's because I wish to God that I could be so painfully oblivious to everyone else in my life. So completely unfeeling and uncaring!

FIRST ACTOR: Uncaring? Did you hear what I said? I can finally get us out of this hole!

SECOND ACTOR: And take us where? Another city? Another beautiful house? Another 'perfect life'…which will fall apart in six months, when you decide to quit this latest dream job for whatever ridiculous reason this time.

FIRST ACTOR: That's not fair.

SECOND ACTOR: No, it's not fair. But it's accurate. You won't like the desk they give you. Your bosses will be morons. Your coworkers will have it in for you. Maybe they'll suddenly stop telling you how wonderful you are three times a day.

FIRST ACTOR: It's not my fault.

SECOND ACTOR: It never is. Someone else will get the better parking spot and that'll push you over the edge. Or maybe you'll just get bored, thinking you don't need this. Thinking you can do better.

FIRST ACTOR: It won't be like that this time…

SECOND ACTOR: That's what you say every time. But in six months, you'll find one excuse or another to get pissed off and quit. You'll walk out, cursing the people who gave you this chance. And then it'll start all over again. The drinking. The bitterness. The self-pity. The bill collectors and eviction notices. And then we end up in another pig sty in another town built on your shattered dreams and inflated ego…

FIRST ACTOR: It won't be like that. I promise.

SECOND ACTOR: Sure.

FIRST ACTOR: Really. This time it'll be different.

SECOND ACTOR: Yeah…Congratulations. I'll go pack. *(Exits)*

FIRST ACTOR: *(Calling out)* It'll be different! You'll see! This time, it'll be different!

27.

FIRST ACTOR: You can't be mad at him forever, you know.

SECOND ACTOR: Who says?

FIRST ACTOR: You've got to let it go.

SECOND ACTOR: Leave me alone.

FIRST ACTOR: It wasn't his fault.

SECOND ACTOR: Then whose fault was it?

FIRST ACTOR: What are you saying?

SECOND ACTOR: He made the choice. He could have said no.

FIRST ACTOR: How can you say that?

SECOND ACTOR: He could have said no.

FIRST ACTOR: He was doing his job.

SECOND ACTOR: He abandoned his family. We needed him…I needed him… I needed him, and he left us alone. Probably didn't give us a second thought.

FIRST ACTOR: Maybe he didn't. Maybe all he thought about was the fire and all those people in danger. How terrified they were. He was thinking of others more than himself. That's what heroes do.

SECOND ACTOR: He should have been thinking of me.

FIRST ACTOR: Maybe he was. Maybe he was thinking how he wanted to be someone his kid could look up to. Someone his son could be proud of.

SECOND ACTOR: That's stupid.

FIRST ACTOR: Is it? You know your Dad. You know how much you meant to him. *(Gently)* Maybe he couldn't live with the look in your eyes, if you knew he turned his back on all those people just when they needed him most. Maybe more than anything…he needed to be a hero to his son. He needed to be a hero for you.

SECOND ACTOR: *(Crying)* But I don't want a hero. I want a dad. A dad who's here... A dad who's alive...

FIRST ACTOR: I know, honey... I know...

28.

FIRST ACTOR: I've given it a lot of thought... and I've decided...

SECOND ACTOR: Decided what?

FIRST ACTOR: I'm not going to kill you. Not yet, anyway.

SECOND ACTOR: I appreciate it. You're a good person.

FIRST ACTOR: No, I'm not. And neither are you. At least I know who I am. What I am.

SECOND ACTOR: Yeah. I've always admired how in touch with your feelings you are.

FIRST ACTOR: Don't try to play me. And don't think I've forgotten. Or that I'll ever get to the point of trusting you again. But you were just lucky enough to marry my little sister. And that got you just one more chance to keep your legs. But just one. You understand?

SECOND ACTOR: Absolutely. You can count on me. Straight and narrow from now on.

FIRST ACTOR: Maybe... Consider yourself on probation. But one mistake, just one wrong move...and they'll be finding pieces of you scattered across three states.

SECOND ACTOR: That seems fair. Don't worry. Straight and narrow from now on.

(First Actor throws a long, dangerous look, then exits. Second Actor pulls out a phone)

SECOND ACTOR: Yeah. It's me. There's something I need you to handle... And I want it messy. Really messy...

29.

FIRST ACTOR: I'm so sorry.

SECOND ACTOR: For what?

FIRST ACTOR: I can't tell you. I feel really bad about it and everything, but I can't tell you.

SECOND ACTOR: You can't tell me what you're sorry for?

FIRST ACTOR: I'm sorry. I can't.

SECOND ACTOR: Then I don't believe it.

FIRST ACTOR: How can you say that? Look how torn up I am! My stomach is tied up in knots. I'm almost shaking with remorse! And look at my face. This is my sorry face. How can you not believe I'm sorry?

SECOND ACTOR: If you were really sorry, you couldn't help but tell me what you did. You'd be open and honest, and just spill your guts like a wino drinking turpentine. You'd be so miserable, you'd confess to everything.

FIRST ACTOR: But I'm miserable!

SECOND ACTOR: Yes, you are. But again, if you were really, really sorry...never-do-it-again, heartbroken and contrite-type of sorry... you would fall to your knees and beg for forgiveness. You'd tell me the truth and then grovel.

FIRST ACTOR: You want me to grovel?

SECOND ACTOR: I don't think that's asking a lot...especially after what you did.

FIRST ACTOR: You don't even know what I did.

SECOND ACTOR: All the more reason for groveling.

FIRST ACTOR: Sorry. I don't grovel.

SECOND ACTOR: If you don't grovel, then clearly you are not sorry about what you did.

FIRST ACTOR:	*(Considers this)* You're right. You're absolutely right. I'm not sorry. In fact, because of your attitude, I'm starting to feel pretty good about what I did. Thank you so much for helping me get in touch with my feelings.
SECOND ACTOR:	What? You're not sorry? You're not going to tell me what you did?!
FIRST ACTOR:	Sorry. *(Exits)*

30.

FIRST ACTOR:	Goodbye.
SECOND ACTOR:	No. I'm not leaving.
FIRST ACTOR:	Please….
SECOND ACTOR:	No. You can't push me away. You can't freeze me out. I promised you years ago I would be in this for the long haul. Not only for all the good and shiny moments, but for the screams and tears and times we couldn't stand each other as well. All of it.
FIRST ACTOR:	It won't help.
SECOND ACTOR:	It's not about help. It's about commitment. It's about being there for each other. Look, I know what's going on… I know all those scared and broken pieces inside you. I know the pain you're feeling. But I can help. I can help you handle the hurt. Help you fix all that's broken inside.
FIRST ACTOR:	You can't.
SECOND ACTOR:	I can. If you'll only let me in.
FIRST ACTOR:	I'm in love with someone else.
SECOND ACTOR:	*(Pause, then…)* Goodbye.

31.

FIRST ACTOR: How could you do that?

SECOND ACTOR: Do what?

FIRST ACTOR: Stop it. Just lose the innocent act. I looked at the books. There's more than half a million dollars missing from the business.

SECOND ACTOR: And you think it was me?

FIRST ACTOR: Who else could it be? You were the only one who had access to the accounts.

SECOND ACTOR: That's just like you. Always blaming me. Everything's my fault!

FIRST ACTOR: *(reading from paper)* Check Number 2713. Nine thousand dollars to your personal account. Check 2804. Six thousand dollars to your personal account. Check 2890. Twelve thousand dollars to your personal account.

SECOND ACTOR: Those were reimbursements for business expenses!

FIRST ACTOR: A total of three hundred and forty thousand? You already have an expense account through the company. And that's not even counting the cash balances that haven't added up for the last three years.

SECOND ACTOR: Why are you doing this?

FIRST ACTOR: Why am *I* doing this? You were the one who ran the business into the ground. You were the one bouncing checks and hiding money. You stole from Mom. From Dad. From me, and even from your own children! What happened to you? What kind of person does that?

SECOND ACTOR: You've always been out to get me. You've always wanted the business for yourself!

FIRST ACTOR: There's nothing left of the business! You made sure of that! Bouncing so many checks, no bank will give us credit.

SECOND ACTOR: If you look at the ledgers and…

FIRST ACTOR: Don't deny it. I have proof. Receipts. Bank statements. You emptied the cash accounts, cheated vendors and drove it into the ground! Even the IRS is after us for the taxes you 'forgot' to pay over the past three year.

SECOND ACTOR: I don't have to listen to this! If you're so smart. You run the company. I'm going home. And you better not spread these lies to my kids.

FIRST ACTOR: I won't have to. I turned your books over to the Sheriff's Department. They froze your bank accounts and issued a warrant for your arrest. Embezzlement. Malfeasance. Tax fraud.

SECOND ACTOR: You son of a… I trusted you!

FIRST ACTOR: Yeah. Trust. That's a good one. *(Turns away)*

SECOND ACTOR: I trusted you! I trusted you!

32.

FIRST ACTOR: I'm not going to do this.

SECOND ACTOR: What do you mean?

FIRST ACTOR: I can't. I keep thinking about her and I just freeze up all over again. I'm not going to do this.

SECOND ACTOR: You have to.

FIRST ACTOR: You were there. You saw it all. How do you expect me to go through with this after what she did to me?

SECOND ACTOR: Because that's how we'll show her. That's how we'll prove she doesn't have that hold on both of us anymore.

FIRST ACTOR: What do you mean, both of us?

SECOND ACTOR: What makes you think you were the only one?

33.

FIRST ACTOR: It's time.

SECOND ACTOR: Give me a few more minutes.

FIRST ACTOR: I'm sorry. It can't wait any longer. Look…I know this isn't going to be easy for you. I know you're worried about what they are going to say.

SECOND ACTOR: Not to my face. They're too polite for that. I'm worried about what they'll say behind my back.

FIRST ACTOR: What does it matter? People love a good scandal. Your real friends will stick beside you.

SECOND ACTOR: What if they're afraid to? What if I don't have any real friends?

FIRST ACTOR: I'll stick beside you. I'm not afraid.

SECOND ACTOR: Thanks. I really mean it. Thanks.

FIRST ACTOR: Don't mention it. Now let's go.

SECOND ACTOR: I…I can't do it. I just can't go out there.

FIRST ACTOR: Maybe not. But *we* can go out there *together*. We'll stick out our chins, slap on a smile and hit 'em with our best, "I dare you to say something" look. *(Smiles)* After that, we'll run like crazy.

SECOND ACTOR: Why are you doing this for me?

FIRST ACTOR: You'd do it for me.

SECOND ACTOR: No, I wouldn't.

FIRST ACTOR: Okay, maybe you wouldn't. But that doesn't matter. I care about you. And this is what people who care about each other do. This is what I do.

SECOND ACTOR: I owe you one, you know.

FIRST ACTOR: Darn right. You owe me big time. Now let's go before I change my mind…

34.

FIRST ACTOR: Oh, my God. I just heard. How are you doing?

SECOND ACTOR: Okay.

FIRST ACTOR: Really okay? Or barely holding on okay?

SECOND ACTOR: I'm... I...

FIRST ACTOR: *(Hugs her)* Oh, sweetie. It'll be all right.

SECOND ACTOR: How? How will it be all right?! Every time I love somebody, they leave me. What is it about me? Am I that hard to love? Am I?

FIRST ACTOR: No, honey. It's not you. Eddie was an idiot. He didn't know what he had.

SECOND ACTOR: He knew what he had. He just wanted something else. Something better...

FIRST ACTOR: He won't find better. He may find younger, trampier, richer, or with bigger boobs, but there's no way he'll ever find anyone as smart, loving and supportive as you.

SECOND ACTOR: Maybe. But he'll have fun looking.

FIRST ACTOR: For a while. And then he's going to realize everything he lost. And that's when he's going to come crawling home, begging you to take him back.

SECOND ACTOR: You think so?

FIRST ACTOR: Absolutely. And if you even think about giving that cheating loser another chance, I will personally kick your self-pitying butt down the block. Got it?

SECOND ACTOR: Got it...

FIRST ACTOR: Good. Now we need ice cream. Lots and lots of ice cream. It's therapeutic.

35.

FIRST ACTOR: I really don't want to learn any more about picking pockets, three-card Monty or how to stack a deck.

SECOND ACTOR: The deck is always stacked, sweetheart. It's either stacked by you, or against you. In this world, you are either a shark or a mark. It's your choice.

FIRST ACTOR: That's your world. In mine, things aren't so cold-blooded. And fathers do more than just show up every six months for fast talk and felony lessons. In my world, you can trust people.

SECOND ACTOR: Then your world is wrong.

FIRST ACTOR: Maybe. Or maybe it's just a world you know absolutely nothing about.

SECOND ACTOR: Sweetheart...

FIRST ACTOR: I gotta go. I'm meeting some friends at the mall.

SECOND ACTOR: You know I love you, don't you?

FIRST ACTOR: I know, Dad. But in your screwed-up world, does that make me the mark...or you?

36.

FIRST ACTOR: Tell me you love me.

SECOND ACTOR: I love you.

FIRST ACTOR: Unh-unh. I don't buy that. There was no sincerity. No warmth. And I had to tell you to tell me you loved me. How can you expect me to believe that?

SECOND ACTOR: I don't. Because the truth is, I don't love you at all. Never did. Never will.

FIRST ACTOR: What? How could you possibly not love me? Everybody loves me!

SECOND ACTOR: No. Everybody tolerates you. Everybody smiles to your face, but giggles at you behind your back. Believe me, I know. I'm one of the gigglers.

FIRST ACTOR: How can you say something like that? How can you be so hurtful?

SECOND ACTOR: Because I love you. *(Turns to leave)* See ya!!

37.

FIRST ACTOR: You're amazing.

SECOND ACTOR: Right.

FIRST ACTOR: No, I mean it. You exude this charm and style and a special… I don't know what to call it. A sparkle, I guess. That's it. You sparkle.

SECOND ACTOR: Right. I sparkle, and you shovel.

FIRST ACTOR: You really don't know how spectacular you are, do you? What a great heart you have. How you are such a tremendously giving person.

SECOND ACTOR: You're broke again, aren't you?

FIRST ACTOR: That has nothing to do with it. I'm being one hundred percent sincere.

SECOND ACTOR: And I'm being one hundred percent played. Don't think I don't realize it. Don't think I don't know every single game of yours.

FIRST ACTOR: That's what is so amazing about you! You are so perceptive!

SECOND ACTOR: My wallet is in the left-hand drawer. Try to leave me enough to buy food this week.

FIRST ACTOR: Thanks. *(Walking away)* You really are amazing.

38.

FIRST ACTOR: It isn't fair, you know.

SECOND ACTOR: No, it isn't.

FIRST ACTOR: I mean, some people live to their seventies. Their eighties. Even their nineties!

SECOND ACTOR: And we don't.

FIRST ACTOR: And we don't. They get to get married. Maybe divorced and remarried again. They get to have kids and grandkids. Big family cookouts with everybody laughing and arguing and stuffing their faces...

SECOND ACTOR: Careers and vacations and retirements...

FIRST ACTOR: They get to wipe away tears. Hold someone close at night. Have someone hold them when the world gets to be too much.

SECOND ACTOR: And we don't.

FIRST ACTOR: It isn't fair.

SECOND ACTOR: I know.

FIRST ACTOR: Would you do it again? Go over there to fight?

SECOND ACTOR: It was the right thing to do.

FIRST ACTOR: But what good did it do? Any of it?

SECOND ACTOR: What do you mean?

FIRST ACTOR: Everything we sacrificed...And they are still killing each other over that same stupid piece of dirt.

SECOND ACTOR: *(Softly)* It was the right thing to do at the time.

FIRST ACTOR: I guess. *(Beat)* You think they'll remember us?

SECOND ACTOR: For a while, I guess... Then only on holidays. A couple of times a year. Then, not at all. *(Sighs)* That's life. For them, anyway.

FIRST ACTOR: Yeah. It isn't fair...

39.

FIRST ACTOR:	This is the last time I'm going to tell you.
SECOND ACTOR:	That's what you said the last time.
FIRST ACTOR:	This time, I mean it.
SECOND ACTOR:	You said that the last time. too. And the time before that. And the time before that.
FIRST ACTOR:	That's it. I'm done. We're through!
SECOND ACTOR:	Another golden oldie. From the memorable November break-up. Or was it the summer slump?
FIRST ACTOR:	I'm serious. I've had it! I just can't take it anymore.
SECOND ACTOR:	Ahhh. 2017. From the legendary, "You're not worth my time" speech. A classic.
FIRST ACTOR:	You disgust me.
SECOND ACTOR:	Hmmm. That one may be new.
FIRST ACTOR:	Well, try this one on for size… I want you out of my sight. Out of my life. I never want to see your face or hear your name ever again.
SECOND ACTOR:	Really?
FIRST ACTOR:	Really. Get out. Now. It's the last time I'm going to tell you.
SECOND ACTOR:	Whew. For a second there, I thought you were serious. Then you went into summer reruns and…
FIRST ACTOR:	Get out!!!!

40.

FIRST ACTOR: Can you move your stuff out of the hallway? I can't get to my front door.

SECOND ACTOR: I'm sorry. Chaotic old me. I'll have this shoved in my apartment before you can say 'annoying neighbor.'

FIRST ACTOR: You're new.

SECOND ACTOR: No, I'm old. Just new to this building. New to living alone after all these years. New to being the new guy. *(Pause)* But um, evidently not new to awkward and uncomfortable conversations with new people I meet.

FIRST ACTOR: Clearly.

SECOND ACTOR: Honestly, some people think I'm funny. I used to have a sense of humor.

FIRST ACTOR: I guess you forgot to pack it.

SECOND ACTOR: Hey, you're funny too.

FIRST ACTOR: Me? I'm just taking out the trash.

SECOND ACTOR: You are taking out your trash while I'm moving in mine. Kind of ironic, don't you think?

FIRST ACTOR: Looks like we circled back to that awkward conversation again.

SECOND ACTOR: Sorry. Did I say sorry before? And here I am saying it again and acting like a sorry excuse for a neighbor. Don't worry. I'm not a serial killer or Grand Master Geek, or something…

FIRST ACTOR: Chill. Stop trying so hard. It's cool.

SECOND ACTOR: I'm chill. I'm cool. I'm so cool I'm chilly. Although that may be the crappy heaters in this apartment building. That was me being funny again. Am I trying too hard?

FIRST ACTOR: Uh-huh.

SECOND ACTOR: And you probably think I'm a complete loser and waste of biomass at this point?

FIRST ACTOR: The jury is still out on that one. That was me being funny, by the way. Listen, we've all been there. Newly single after a relationship we thought was perfect shreds our soul. Suddenly, forced to get a new address and new friends, to hide the embarrassment of explaining to the old ones why it didn't work out with the former love of our life. So, you ratchet up the energy to hide the humiliation, and end up being twice as humiliated by discovering how hard it is to reconnect with people when you feel like a complete and utter loser.

SECOND ACTOR: Wow. When you take out the trash, you really take out the trash.

FIRST ACTOR: Like I said, we've all been there.

SECOND ACTOR: Tell me... Does it get any easier?

FIRST ACTOR: Not really. But wine helps. I have some in my apartment. That is, if I ever could get to my door.

SECOND ACTOR: Oh, sorry, I...let me get this out of your way. Hey, was that an invitation? The wine thing, I mean?

FIRST ACTOR: Move your crap out of the hall, Grand Master Geek. I'll have a bottle uncorked in ten. We can get smashed and swap horrendous ex stories. I guarantee I'll win.

SECOND ACTOR: Clean hallway in five. Uncorked wine in ten. Exes going down in flames shortly thereafter. I love this building! Wait a minute. Do you have a name?

FIRST ACTOR: Yes.

SECOND ACTOR: Okay.... Uh, that was you being either funny or ironic again, wasn't it? Wasn't it?

FIRST ACTOR: Don't make me let the wine breathe too much. See you in ten. *(Exits)*

SECOND ACTOR: I'm gonna love this building!

41.

FIRST ACTOR: I knew it was you.

SECOND ACTOR: Knew what was me?

FIRST ACTOR: Don't play the innocent. I know what kind of back-stabbing snake you really are.

SECOND ACTOR: Actually, snakes don't have arms. Therefore, it would be impossible for them to stab someone in the back. Or the front, for that matter.

FIRST ACTOR: Being cute isn't going to get you out of this.

SECOND ACTOR: Get me out of what? I honestly have no idea what you're talking about.

FIRST ACTOR: Do you think I'm that stupid? Do you?

SECOND ACTOR: How am I supposed to answer that? Yes, I think you're that stupid, which will make you even madder at me… or no, I don't think you're stupid…which would be a complete and utter lie. But then again, you're probably too stupid to notice.

FIRST ACTOR: Maybe, you're right. Maybe I am stupid. Stupid for thinking you could ever be trusted. Stupid for believing you were ever my friend.

SECOND ACTOR: Don't expect me to disagree with you here.

FIRST ACTOR: *(Smiles)* But at least I'm not stupid enough to let you marry her. You may have ruined my life, but I won't let you ruin hers, too.

SECOND ACTOR: What's really stupid is that you think you can stop me. That you think she'll even listen to you. Remember, she's almost as stupid as you are. Not quite, but almost.

FIRST ACTOR: She doesn't have to listen to me… *(Pulls out a phone)* She just listened to you.

SECOND ACTOR: You're lying. She's not on the phone.

FIRST ACTOR: *(Into phone)* Can you hear him now? *(Back to Second Actor)* Gotta love the reception with these new phones. *(Into phone)* Yeah. It was a stupid thing to say. What did you ever see in him anyway? *(Exits)*

42.

FIRST ACTOR: Did you tell him?

SECOND ACTOR: I wanted to.

FIRST ACTOR: But you didn't.

SECOND ACTOR: I couldn't. I looked at his face, and... I... I just couldn't.

FIRST ACTOR: You have to tell him.

SECOND ACTOR: I know.

FIRST ACTOR: It isn't fair. Isn't fair to either of them.

SECOND ACTOR: Don't you think I know that?! Don't you think I beat myself up every day over this?

FIRST ACTOR: Glad to hear that. But it still doesn't solve the problem. You know that when they find out, it's going to absolutely destroy them. They trusted you. We all did.

SECOND ACTOR: I know. What would you do?

FIRST ACTOR: Me? I would never have been that stupid. Or gotten in this deep. But if I did, I'd probably kill myself. Kill myself in the most messy and painful way possible. Something Medieval, I think. I'll be happy to give you suggestions.

SECOND ACTOR: You're too kind.

43.

FIRST ACTOR: So how do we do this?

SECOND ACTOR: That depends on the statement you want to make.

FIRST ACTOR: The statement? What statement?

SECOND ACTOR: Something like this always makes a statement. You want to be remembered. You want to get back at all those who were mean to you. All the people who didn't appreciate you enough.

FIRST ACTOR: Well, yeah.

SECOND ACTOR: You want them to feel guilty. You want the world to realize that you were way too good for it.

FIRST ACTOR: Okay. That sounds good. Nobody appreciated me, and I am too good for the world. Way too good.

SECOND ACTOR: No doubt. And everyone will realize that once this is over.

FIRST ACTOR: Especially my exes. They all better realize that.

SECOND ACTOR: *(writing a note)* Anguish for the Exes. Check.

FIRST ACTOR: I mean I want them to really cry. Rend their clothes and gnash their teeth. Real Old Testament-type wailing. Make them feel miserable for years. Decades!

SECOND ACTOR: Hmmm. Miserable for decades usually requires something dramatic.

FIRST ACTOR: What do you mean, dramatic?

SECOND ACTOR: Something messy. And really, really painful.

FIRST ACTOR: Ulp, Is that necessary?

SECOND ACTOR: If you want decades of unrelenting guilt and sorrow, then yes.

FIRST ACTOR: How painful are we talking about?

SECOND ACTOR: Well, we have lots of options. We can throw your body into an industrial woodchipper. Have you fall over a guard rail at the zoo and be devoured by hungry lions or polar bears. Swallow a half-bottle of Drano. Have you dragged under the wheels of a semi-truck for half a mile, or so. You know, the old standards.

FIRST ACTOR: I'm not sure any of those work for me. I'm not real good with pain.

SECOND ACTOR: Then you may want one of our Premiere Options. Messy, but Instantaneous.

FIRST ACTOR: How instantaneous?

SECOND ACTOR: You never see it coming. And you're dead before you know it.

FIRST ACTOR: That doesn't sound too bad. Give me a few examples.

SECOND ACTOR: Falling down an elevator shaft. Accidental clothesline decapitation. Grenade in your underwear drawer.

FIRST ACTOR: Won't all of those make me look a little…I don't know…stupid?

SECOND ACTOR: Probably. But you'll be splattered into a million pieces. You won't care.

FIRST ACTOR: Maybe this wasn't such a great idea…

SECOND ACTOR: Hey, you're the one who called the Suicide Hot Line!

FIRST ACTOR: But I thought you guys were supposed to talk me *out of* committing suicide.

SECOND ACTOR: That's a common misconception many people have. Now, back to the business at hand. How do you feel about razor blades and poisonous snakes?

FIRST ACTOR: No way. This all sounds terrible! I would rather live and be miserable than listen to your crazy ideas about killing myself! I'm outta here! *(Exits)*

SECOND ACTOR: *(smiling)* Works every time.

44.

FIRST ACTOR: This is awful.

SECOND ACTOR: I know.

FIRST ACTOR: I've never felt so frustrated. So confused...

SECOND ACTOR: I can imagine.

FIRST ACTOR: After all these years, I finally find the perfect person...

SECOND ACTOR: I'm not perfect.

FIRST ACTOR: You are perfect to me. Perfect for me.

SECOND ACTOR: That's a pretty high pedestal you're putting me up on. And I'm afraid of heights.

FIRST ACTOR: See? That shows how perfect we are together! You even have my sense of humor.

SECOND ACTOR: You are the only one who seems to appreciate it.

FIRST ACTOR: I do. I appreciate everything about you. That's what's killing me. I finally find someone who thinks like I do. Somebody who shares my hopes and dreams and deepest desires. I finally find the one person I want to spend the rest of my life with...and it's all wrong.

SECOND ACTOR: Worse than wrong. It's impossible.

FIRST ACTOR: Don't say that. I don't mind the age gap. Or the fact that we're a thousand miles apart.

SECOND ACTOR: That's one long day's drive. Three hours on a plane.

FIRST ACTOR: Exactly. And it's okay with me that you have kids.

SECOND ACTOR: My kids are my life.

FIRST ACTOR: I admire that about you! I don't even mind that you're married...

SECOND ACTOR: You should.

FIRST ACTOR: I know I should. But I don't. None of it matters, because you and I have this incredible, impossible, irresistible connection. You are my soulmate. We were made for each other!

SECOND ACTOR: Not really.

FIRST ACTOR: You know it's true. Everything else is just details. But the worst part is…my perfect person…the one I am so hopelessly, obsessively in love with…is a fictional character.

SECOND ACTOR: Well, there is that.

FIRST ACTOR: The most wonderfully written, fleshed out character I've ever seen! I must have seen that movie twenty, twenty-five times. And every time, I fall in love with you even more.

SECOND ACTOR: It's not right to love a fictional character. What would people say?

FIRST ACTOR: I don't care! It doesn't matter to me what anybody thinks. I don't care how crazy it is. You are perfect. Perfectly perfect. I refuse to let you go!

SECOND ACTOR: I'm pretty sure therapy is in order here. Or some serious medication.

FIRST ACTOR: I am going to make this work. You and me. I'm going to find a way.

SECOND ACTOR: Good luck with that.

FIRST ACTOR: Crap! It's almost seven! If I leave now, I can just make it in time to catch your next showing! See you on the big screen, my love. My sweetheart! My soulmate! *(Exits)*

SECOND ACTOR: *(Sighs)* Therapy. Mega therapy.

45.

FIRST ACTOR: Hi.

SECOND ACTOR: Good. I'm glad you came.

FIRST ACTOR: *(Clutching a crumpled piece of paper)* I got your letter.

SECOND ACTOR: Yeah.

FIRST ACTOR: Did you mean this? Is this just some kind of joke? Because it's not funny. It's really not funny, you know?

SECOND ACTOR: Look. I didn't mean to hurt you, but…

FIRST ACTOR: But you decided to anyway.

SECOND ACTOR: I'm sorry. I don't know what else to say.

FIRST ACTOR: Say you don't mean this! You don't mean any of it. It was all a mistake and we can start over. It can be just like it was before. *We* can be just like before.

SECOND ACTOR: I can't say that. It'll never be like that again. We both know that.

FIRST ACTOR: We don't know that. *I* don't know that. All I know is that I love you. More than the world. And you love me, too. You know you love me.

SECOND ACTOR: I don't. I…I'm sorry.

FIRST ACTOR: You don't love me?

SECOND ACTOR: That's what I've been trying to tell you. But you never listen. You never listen to anything I say. Anything at all.

FIRST ACTOR: I do listen. But you're wrong. You do love me. I can see it in your eyes. I can feel it in your chest when you hold me. You can't fake something like that.

SECOND ACTOR: No, you can't. But it's not love. It's not.

FIRST ACTOR: Then what is it? Look in my eyes and tell me what you feel when you look at me.

SECOND ACTOR: *(Pause, then…)* Pity.

FIRST ACTOR: *(Pause. Let's this sink in)* I…I have to go…
SECOND ACTOR: Look, I'm sorry. I really didn't mean to hurt you.
FIRST ACTOR: You know…you could have said anything else. Anything else in the world, except pity… And if that's what you really feel, you could have lied. *(Exiting)* That would have been the kind thing to do.

46.

FIRST ACTOR: Is this seat taken? *(No reply)* Mind if I sit here? *(No reply)* Thanks. So, how are you? *(no reply)* Not much of a talker, are you?
SECOND ACTOR: I…I'm waiting for someone.
FIRST ACTOR: That's nice. Family? Friend? High school sweetheart? *(Second Actor shakes head. Says nothing)* Look. I'm sorry. I didn't mean to pry. I can see that I'm bothering you. It's just that I'm new in town and I don't know anyone. Not a single person for five hundred miles. It gets kind of lonely, you know? *(No reply)* As I said, I'm sorry. If you want me to go away, I will. *(No reply. Gets up to leave)* Anyway… take care.
SECOND ACTOR: Um… Where…?
FIRST ACTOR: Where what?
SECOND ACTOR: Where…did you say you were from?
FIRST ACTOR: Pittsburgh. I'm from Pittsburgh. Ever been there?
SECOND ACTOR: No.
FIRST ACTOR: You'd like it. So, tell me a little about yourself?

47.

FIRST ACTOR: She deserved better.

SECOND ACTOR: Uh huh.

FIRST ACTOR: I'm serious. Nobody should go out like that.

SECOND ACTOR: Yeah? And how should they go out?

FIRST ACTOR: I dunno. Peaceful. In their sleep. Nice glass of wine. Get a little tired. Lay down. And then never wake up again. That's the way it should go.

SECOND ACTOR: Yeah. But that would put us out of business. Our clients prefer it bloody.

FIRST ACTOR: I guess. *(Sighs)* Gets to you though, doesn't it?

SECOND ACTOR: Not really. It's a job. We do what we have to do.

FIRST ACTOR: Don't tell me it doesn't it get to you. Don't you ever ask yourself, who was she? What did she do that was so wrong? Who did she cross to have to suffer that much?

SECOND ACTOR: It's not for us to know. Best not to think about it.

FIRST ACTOR: Sometimes I can't help it. *(Stands)* Look, I'm gonna grab a beer. You want one?

SECOND ACTOR: Sure. *(Watches First Actor exit. Pulls out a phone and speed dials)* Yeah. It's done. But I'm worried about the new guy. Looks like he's gonna be a problem. *(Pause)* Don't worry. I'll handle it. *(Hangs up)*

FIRST ACTOR: *(Enters, with two beers)* I dunno know, man. It still kinda gets to me...

SECOND ACTOR: Just sleep on it, brother. I guarantee, come morning, you'll never talk about it again. *(They clink beers and drink)*

48.

FIRST ACTOR: Seriously? This again?

SECOND ACTOR: What again? I don't know what you're talking about.

FIRST ACTOR: Don't you give me that! I am so not in the mood this morning.

SECOND ACTOR: I didn't say anything. I was eating my cereal.

FIRST ACTOR: Don't give me that. It was the way you were eating your cereal. Loudly. Judgmentally.

SECOND ACTOR: It's Cap'n Crunch. He's crispy, not judgmental.

FIRST ACTOR: You think I'm wrong. That I'm responsible for what happened?

SECOND ACTOR: I don't think that at all. Neither does Cap'n Crunch. We just want a nice quiet breakfast.

FIRST ACTOR: Oh? And I'm stopping you from having a nice quiet breakfast?

SECOND ACTOR: Does that even deserve an answer?

FIRST ACTOR: What do you mean by that?

SECOND ACTOR: It's eight-thirty and you're already clocking in at forty-three complaints per hour. I didn't make the bed. Didn't hang up my towels right. You don't like the way that dress looks on you. The weatherman is a moronic liar. And I chew judgmentally.

FIRST ACTOR: I…I'm sorry. I know I've been taking it out on you. Ever since… Ever since he…

SECOND ACTOR: I know. I hate it, too. *(Pause)* Sorry if I was crunching judgmentally.

49.

FIRST ACTOR: Don't lie to me.

SECOND ACTOR: I would never lie to you. You know that.

FIRST ACTOR: Maybe…but how do I really know? I mean, if you were lying to me…if you have been lying to me from the beginning…the most obvious thing to say would be 'I would never lie to you."

SECOND ACTOR: And if I'm telling the truth…like I have been from the start…the most obvious thing to say would be 'I would never lie to you."

FIRST ACTOR: So, I guess I'll never know for sure.

SECOND ACTOR: Of course, you know. You've always known. It doesn't matter what I say.

FIRST ACTOR: Yeah. The question is…now that I know…what do I do with that?

50.

FIRST ACTOR: I need you.

SECOND ACTOR: Of course, you do. Too bad you never realized how much until now. When it's too late.

FIRST ACTOR: What do you mean, 'too late?'

SECOND ACTOR: I'm not sure I need you anymore.

FIRST ACTOR: Of course, you do. I can see it in your eyes. The way you look at me. The way your lip quivers, when you're trying to look so tough. So strong. You need me…and you hate that about yourself.

SECOND ACTOR: There are lots of things I hate about myself. Needing you isn't one of them. Needing you completely out of my life is.

FIRST ACTOR: If you keep talking like that, one of these days, I might believe you.

51.

FIRST ACTOR: What are you doing? Why are you sitting here in the dark?

SECOND ACTOR: I'm thinking.

FIRST ACTOR: Do I even have to ask about what?

SECOND ACTOR: I miss her.

FIRST ACTOR: I know. Me too.

SECOND ACTOR: She was always such a fighter. I never thought she would go so quickly. It was hard to watch. For the longest time, I never thought she would go at all.

FIRST ACTOR: I know.

SECOND ACTOR: But it happened so fast. The way the life just seemed to slip right out of her. A little more each day. Until she looked so fragile. So empty...

FIRST ACTOR: These things happen. We don't know why.

SECOND ACTOR: It's funny. I can't even remember her not being sick. All those years she was healthy and all I can remember is her in the hospital those last two weeks. I can't even remember what her laugh sounded like. Isn't that strange?

FIRST ACTOR: She had a great laugh. She used to laugh a lot.

FIRST ACTOR: Yeah. But it's like remembering a TV show you saw a long time ago. You can only vaguely recall the sound of their voices. Or even why you used to love the show so much in the first place...

FIRST ACTOR: She loved us. You know that.

FIRST ACTOR: I know. But I miss her.

FIRST ACTOR: Me too.

52.

FIRST ACTOR: Okay. It's done. Just like you said.

SECOND ACTOR: It's over?

FIRST ACTOR: Yeah. You don't have to worry anymore.

SECOND ACTOR: You're sure about that?

FIRST ACTOR: I'm sure.

SECOND ACTOR: But what if, one day...?

FIRST ACTOR: *(angrily)* Hey, I told you it's over! You got what you wanted! Let's just leave it at that, okay?!

SECOND ACTOR: It's not that I don't believe you...

FIRST ACTOR: Right.

SECOND ACTOR: I just have to be sure.

(First Actor tosses a large crumpled bag in her lap)

SECOND ACTOR: What's this?

FIRST ACTOR: Be sure.

(Second Actor opens the bag. Her face turns pale. She gasps in a torn, staccato breath)

SECOND ACTOR: The money...it's in the kitchen. In the junk drawer. Under the...um, duct tape and old batteries. *(First Actor nods. Turns to exit)* Hey, you do know that I love you, don't you?

FIRST ACTOR: So you said...

(First Actor shoots her a withering stare of distilled contempt, then turns and exits.

Second Actor looks to the bag on her lap. Slowly, her expression evolves from deep repulsion to a bone-chilling smile. Carefully places the bag on the floor, then returns to her magazine, far more relaxed now)

53.

FIRST ACTOR: I'm late.

SECOND ACTOR: So, what's new?

FIRST ACTOR: No. I'm really late! I was supposed to be there seven minutes ago!

SECOND ACTOR: Uh-huh.

FIRST ACTOR: I haven't taken a shower yet. I don't have my stuff ready and it's all the way across town!

SECOND ACTOR: Not a good sign.

FIRST ACTOR: What am I going to do?!

SECOND ACTOR: Sorry. I stopped feeling sorry for you twenty-seven lost jobs ago. You don't want to be late? Learn to get up on time. Simple as that.

FIRST ACTOR: I really hate you.

SECOND ACTOR: Uh-huh. You're going to be late.

54.

FIRST ACTOR: I'll do anything to make you happy. Just please…please tell me what you want.

SECOND ACTOR: I don't want a lot. Just someone to listen to my stories.

FIRST ACTOR: I do that. I listen to your stories.

SECOND ACTOR: Someone to care about the things I care about. Someone to hold me through the night…

FIRST ACTOR: But I do all that!

SECOND ACTOR: I know. Look, the truth is… I just want someone to love me.

FIRST ACTOR: I love you.

SECOND ACTOR: I know… But I want someone…else.

55.

FIRST ACTOR: Thank you for coming today.

SECOND ACTOR: How could I refuse? Besides, I feel I owe you one.

FIRST ACTOR: I am so happy to hear you finally admit that.

SECOND ACTOR: Huh?

FIRST ACTOR: Well, the truth is… you do owe me one. In fact, you owe me several, after all the things I have done for you over the years. I know. I know. There are too many to count. But the important thing is that you finally are showing a little gratitude. That's very mature of you.

SECOND ACTOR: Mature, huh?

FIRST ACTOR: Absolutely. I honestly believed it would be years before you had the capacity to accept that level of responsibility. I am very proud of you.

SECOND ACTOR: Thank you so much. There's one thing I have to ask, if you don't mind?

FIRST ACTOR: Not at all.

SECOND ACTOR: We're you always this much of a jerk?

56.

FIRST ACTOR: How are you feeling?

SECOND ACTOR: Better now. I'm even able to keep some food down.

FIRST ACTOR: I was really worried about you. We all were.

SECOND ACTOR: Then why did you let me drink so much? You know I'm a diabetic. You know what drinking that much could do to me.

FIRST ACTOR: I tried to tell you, but you wouldn't listen.

SECOND ACTOR: I have a drinking problem. What did you expect?! As a friend of mine – a supposed friend - you were supposed to make sure I was okay.

FIRST ACTOR: You are right. I wasn't there for you. I let you down.

SECOND ACTOR: You sure did.

FIRST ACTOR: I feel awful about it.

SECOND ACTOR: You should.

FIRST ACTOR: But problem or not…it still didn't give you the right to burn my house down.

57.

FIRST ACTOR: I owe you my life.

SECOND ACTOR: Don't make such a big deal out of it.

FIRST ACTOR: It is a big deal. I don't know how I can ever repay you.

SECOND ACTOR: Fine. You can't. Let's forget it, okay?

FIRST ACTOR: Forget it? Nobody's ever been that good to me before. I mean, I was stunned. It was the greatest act of generosity I have ever seen!

SECOND ACTOR: Enough. You're welcome. Time to move on.

FIRST ACTOR: Move on? I can't stop thinking about it. You are the kindest, most giving, most selfless human being I've ever met. and I…

SECOND ACTOR: Listen, you idiot! I didn't do it for you! I did it for me. For me! You get that? It had absolutely nothing to do with you. You were just a…a collateral beneficiary. I did it for me. So let's drop it, okay?

FIRST ACTOR: *(Pause, then…)* How can you be so selfish?

58.

FIRST ACTOR: ...And that's exactly what happened.

SECOND ACTOR: Oh, my God! Why did you tell me that?!

FIRST ACTOR: You asked.

SECOND ACTOR: But I didn't know you were going to tell me *that!* You said you had a really juicy secret but couldn't tell me.

FIRST ACTOR: And then, you insisted. You bribed, begged and threatened me. So, I told you. Now *you* have a really juicy secret. One that has to stay secret.

SECOND ACTOR: There is no way. This deserves to be Facebooked! Instagrammed and SnapChatted. At least let me twitter it, okay?

FIRST ACTOR: No. If you say anything. If you post anything, snap or tweet anything, they'll know it came from me.

SECOND ACTOR: But it did come from you.

FIRST ACTOR: Look, do you know who we are dealing with here?

SECOND ACTOR: I just...

FIRST ACTOR: Do you understand what it'll do to them if this gets out? Do you know what they'll do to us if they find out we spread it around?

SECOND ACTOR: Yeah, but you don't think they would...?

FIRST ACTOR: In a heartbeat.

SECOND ACTOR: Oh, my God!

FIRST ACTOR: Exactly.

SECOND ACTOR: Then why did you tell me that?!

59.

FIRST ACTOR: So, this is it?

SECOND ACTOR: Yeah.

FIRST ACTOR: And you're just going to walk away?

SECOND ACTOR: Why not?

FIRST ACTOR: Why not? Because of all that's happened! Because…because it would be an ice-cold thing to do. Because people don't do that to each other.

SECOND ACTOR: People don't do a lot of things we do. That's the problem.

FIRST ACTOR: What does that mean? Are you blaming me now? I asked you a question. Are you blaming me?!

SECOND ACTOR: Yeah.

FIRST ACTOR: So, all this is my fault.

SECOND ACTOR: Not all of it. Some of it. Most of it, I guess.

FIRST ACTOR: You make me sick.

SECOND ACTOR: Yeah. I know.

FIRST ACTOR: I didn't kill him.

SECOND ACTOR: It doesn't matter.

FIRST ACTOR: Accidents happen, you know?

SECOND ACTOR: Yeah.

FIRST ACTOR: Sometimes I really hate you. *(no reply)* I said, sometimes I really hate you!

SECOND ACTOR: I always assumed you would, eventually.

60.

FIRST ACTOR: Is this gonna work?

SECOND ACTOR: Have I ever steered you wrong?

FIRST ACTOR: Not yet.

SECOND ACTOR: And I never will. You can trust me. I'd take a bullet for you.

FIRST ACTOR: A bullet?

SECOND ACTOR: Right in the chest. That's us. I'd let it puncture my lungs and rip open my heart for you.

FIRST ACTOR: But, uh, you don't expect me to take a bullet for you?

SECOND ACTOR: Wouldn't you?

FIRST ACTOR: Honestly, I don't know. I'd like to think I would. But I'd rather not be put in a situation to find out.

SECOND ACTOR: Well, I appreciate the honesty, at least. But don't worry. You just go down that alley and knock on the fourth door. I already told them you'd be coming. They'll take care of you. Trust me.

FIRST ACTOR: They'll take care of me?

SECOND ACTOR: Yeah. Trust me.

61.

FIRST ACTOR: Nothing ever goes as planned, does it?

SECOND ACTOR: No.

FIRST ACTOR: Maybe that's why they say God has a sense of humor.

SECOND ACTOR: More like a vicious streak. Giving us a quick glimpse of 'what could have been' and then yanking the rug right out from under us. *(Bitterly)* Some joke.

FIRST ACTOR: That's just like you. Blaming 'Divine Intervention' for your screw-ups.

SECOND ACTOR: Our screw-ups.

SECOND ACTOR: Okay. Our screw-ups.

SECOND ACTOR: Don't worry. I have a full and detailed list of all my faults and failings burned into the back of my eyelids. You made sure of that. Or I did. What does it matter? Either way, I know I'll have more than a few decades of self-loathing to look forward to.

FIRST ACTOR: It doesn't have to be that way.

SECOND ACTOR: Keep telling yourself that. Kiss the kids goodbye for me.

FIRST ACTOR: Not a chance.

62.

FIRST ACTOR: Who was that on the phone?

SECOND ACTOR: No one. Wrong number or something.

FIRST ACTOR: Or something?

SECOND ACTOR: Why do you always do that? Imply every wrong number is something devious? And assume every time I go out, I'm meeting someone? Why do you have to always blow everything out of proportion like that?

FIRST ACTOR: I'm sorry. I have trust issues. I've had some bad experiences in my life.

SECOND ACTOR: But not with me. I'm on your side, remember?

FIRST ACTOR: Yeah. I'm sorry. I'll do better. I promise.

SECOND ACTOR: Great. Now I have to go to the store to pick up something for dinner.

FIRST ACTOR: Something for dinner?

SECOND ACTOR: That's right.

FIRST ACTOR: *(Pause)* I'll go with you.

63.

FIRST ACTOR: How are you doing?

SECOND ACTOR: Not too bad.

FIRST ACTOR: Holding that razor blade for any particular reason?

SECOND ACTOR: Maybe.

FIRST ACTOR: Maybe is not an answer. Maybe is what you say when you are trying to avoid a conversation. Trying to push people away. Is that what you're trying to do here? Push everyone away?

SECOND ACTOR: Maybe.

FIRST ACTOR: Well, I gotta tell ya, it's not gonna to work on me. So, tell me...are you holding that razor blade for a reason?

SECOND ACTOR: Seems like the thing to do.

FIRST ACTOR: That bad, huh?

SECOND ACTOR: You have to feel something for it to be bad. This isn't bad. This is numb. And numb just ain't worth it.

FIRST ACTOR: And you think that razor is going to help?

SECOND ACTOR: Maybe.

FIRST ACTOR: Maybe doesn't work on me. Remember? *(No reply)* Look, kid, I know about lost and I know about numb. I lived numb for more years than you can imagine.

SECOND ACTOR: I can't imagine living like this for years. Sometimes I can't imagine living at all.

FIRST ACTOR: Grow up, kid. Forget the Shakespeare. Suicide isn't some romantic act. It's taking everything you are and everything you ever could be and turning it into a rotting pile of worm food. If you think that's cool, or hip or profound in some way, then you're not numb. You're just stupid.

SECOND ACTOR: *(Pause)* You know...you'd make a lousy cheerleader.

64.

FIRST ACTOR: It's out there, you know.

SECOND ACTOR: What is?

FIRST ACTOR: Everything. My dreams. My life. Maybe even more than I can imagine.

SECOND ACTOR: Maybe that's your problem. You imagine too much. And live too little.

FIRST ACTOR: What's that supposed to mean?

SECOND ACTOR: I don't know. I don't know anything anymore. I just see words coming out of my mouth and I'm not even sure I understand half of what I say anymore. It's like I talk just to overpower the silence. I've become a social babbler...afraid to be alone with my own thoughts.

FIRST ACTOR: That's okay. Thoughts are overrated. That's why I try not to have any.

SECOND ACTOR: Mission accomplished.

FIRST ACTOR: You do understand why I have to go, don't you?

SECOND ACTOR: Yeah. It's all out there. Destination Dreamland. Ambition Central. Everything you can't find in this sleepy old town.

FIRST ACTOR: That's not exactly the way I'd put it, but...

SECOND ACTOR: No worries. You got places to meet. People to be. I get it. I totally get it.

FIRST ACTOR: Are you going to be okay?

SECOND ACTOR: Me? Sure. I've forgotten about you already.

FIRST ACTOR: Good to know. I was always famous for my forgettability.

SECOND ACTOR: Really? I had forgotten that.

FIRST ACTOR: Most people do. Take care of yourself.

SECOND ACTOR: Yeah. It's what I do best.

65.

FIRST ACTOR: Shut up.

SECOND ACTOR: I didn't say anything.

FIRST ACTOR: You were about to. You were going to complain that this isn't going as planned. That it's falling apart. That we screwed up somehow.

SECOND ACTOR: But I didn't sa…

FIRST ACTOR: You were about to say we're going to get killed doing this. And you don't want to die. Not out here. Not like this. That's what you were gonna say. Wasn't it? Wasn't it?!

SECOND ACTOR: No…yes.…I don't want to die out here… I'm sorry. I don't. Not for this.

FIRST ACTOR: Shut up.

SECOND ACTOR: *(Desperate)* This is wrong, and you know it! Dying for something you believe in is one thing. Dying for no reason at all…just because your cousin's trying to prove how tough he can be…That's just stupid. It's stupid and it's wrong and you know it!

FIRST ACTOR: It doesn't matter what I know. We do as we're told. Now shut up and put your mask on. And make sure you don't shoot me in the back by mistake. Let's go.

66.

FIRST ACTOR: Did he suffer much?

SECOND ACTOR: The doctors say no.

FIRST ACTOR: But you don't believe them?

SECOND ACTOR: I saw what he went through these last four years. I saw how he died piece by piece. I saw the life leak out of him, and what it did to his soul to see it happening.

FIRST ACTOR: I'm sorry I wasn't around to help more.

SECOND ACTOR: Right.

FIRST ACTOR: I couldn't. I just couldn't… It doesn't mean I didn't love him. I just couldn't bear to see him like that. I don't have your strength. I never did.

SECOND ACTOR: Then I don't know who I feel sorrier for. You or him. But if it ever happens to you, I hope there'll be someone left who has the strength to be there with you. Instead of the excuses…

67.

FIRST ACTOR: I've waited my whole life for this.

SECOND ACTOR: Really?

FIRST ACTOR: For as long as I remember, I've been planning for this moment. Working hard for it. Saw a hundred different scenarios of how it would play out. And now here I am! Hard to believe…

SECOND ACTOR: So…was it worth it?

FIRST ACTOR: Of course. Absolutely. No doubt in my mind.

SECOND ACTOR: Then you're even more hopeless than I thought. Wasting so much of your time and energy on something that might or might not happen years down the line.

FIRST ACTOR: But it worked. Here I am. About to take that big step.

SECOND ACTOR: Yeah, but I didn't waste one second of my childhood worrying about this. And now here I am too. Pretty funny, don't you think?

FIRST ACTOR: I hate you.

68.

FIRST ACTOR: She's gone, isn't she?

SECOND ACTOR: She took everything. The light bulb in the closet. Even the last roll of toilet paper.

FIRST ACTOR: That sounds like her.

SECOND ACTOR: That sounds like her now. Not the way she used to be.

FIRST ACTOR: If you're saying I changed her, don't waste your breath. She tried to change me too.

SECOND ACTOR: I know.

FIRST ACTOR: She's gone. I should be happy. Don't you think I should be happy?

SECOND ACTOR: You should be happy...

FIRST ACTOR: Then why aren't I? This is what I wanted. What I pushed for. But now that she's gone...

SECOND ACTOR: ...you're scared.

FIRST ACTOR: I don't know about scared, but...

SECOND ACTOR: You were always scared. Scared you were missing out on something. Scared you were missing out on everything.

FIRST ACTOR: She was just getting a little too much, y'know? Smothering. I just wanted...

SECOND ACTOR: You just wanted it all... The independence. The control. The permission...

FIRST ACTOR: Permission for what?

SECOND ACTOR: For everything. All you kept dreaming about was a stranger's touch, the warmth of new skin and the electricity of an unfamiliar smile. You wanted the freedom to jump at every sidelong glance and chance encounter to see where it might lead.

FIRST ACTOR: Is that too much to ask?

SECOND ACTOR:	It was for her.
FIRST ACTOR:	I was honest with her. I warned her from the start.
SECOND ACTOR:	Served her right then.
FIRST ACTOR:	That's right! I told her I was never going to be that plastic smile in the tux on the top of the wedding cake. I…I like to keep my options open.
SECOND ACTOR:	And now you have nothing but years and years of options ahead of you.
FIRST ACTOR:	I guess…
SECOND ACTOR:	Only now that you're free to have it all, you're afraid there won't be any more new smiles, or glances or chance encounters. Maybe all you are now is alone.
FIRST ACTOR:	So why are you still here?
SECOND ACTOR:	Me? I'm the type who loves to watch the train wreck.

69.

FIRST ACTOR:	Don't look at me. Don't even look at me.
SECOND ACTOR:	I can't help it.
FIRST ACTOR:	Please, just go away.
SECOND ACTOR:	No. This is my house too. No matter what happened, no matter what you're feeling now, you belong to me.
FIRST ACTOR:	I don't belong to anyone. I don't even belong to myself anymore.
SECOND ACTOR:	Don't talk like that.
FIRST ACTOR:	It's true. Everything I believed in is…gone. Just gone.
SECOND ACTOR:	I'm not. I'm right here.
FIRST ACTOR:	That's what makes it so painful.
SECOND ACTOR:	You don't know what pain is. Believe me.
FIRST ACTOR:	Well, whatever this is. I just want it to stop. Okay?

70.

FIRST ACTOR: I'm not going to tell you anything.

SECOND ACTOR: That's what they all say. Right before the screaming starts. It hurts my ears and I have to clean this whole place with bleach afterwards. But I guess everyone has to have that one moment to feel like a hero.

FIRST ACTOR: You don't scare me.

SECOND ACTOR: That's the other thing they always say. But rest assured, I'm not trying to scare you. It hardly matters to me what you think or feel at all. My job is simply to inflict the proper amount of pain to extract the necessary information from you. Anything else is just for fun.

FIRST ACTOR: You're a monster.

SECOND ACTOR: I suppose I am. An efficient one, though. And I usually get results. I am considered very good at my job. That is something these days.

FIRST ACTOR: You don't have to do this.

SECOND ACTOR: Ah, you have now uttered the four basic movie clichés for this type of situation... 'I'm not going to tell you anything.' 'You don't scare me.' 'You're a monster' and 'You don't have to do this.' I hear it all the time. Not necessarily in that order, but I imagine it says something about how cinema affects our society. We have pre-written dialogue for every occasion. Even one as painful as this. Shall we begin?

FIRST ACTOR: That's a cliché too.

SECOND ACTOR: How so?

FIRST ACTOR: 'Shall we begin?' The insane villain always says that just as he picks up a sharp knife or electrodes, hungry rats, or whatever else he's using to torture the good guy.

SECOND ACTOR: Hmmm. You're right. I suppose I am turning into a bit of a cliché myself. But don't think that makes me any less serious about my intentions. And unlike the movies, there won't be any daring rescue at the last possible instant. That never happens in real life, believe me. Oh, and one more thing...

FIRST ACTOR: What's that?

SECOND ACTOR: Which one of us is the villain and which is the good guy depends entirely on the information you are about to give me. Now...shall we begin?

71.

FIRST ACTOR: Why the hell can't I leave you?!

SECOND ACTOR: Excuse me?

FIRST ACTOR: You heard me! Why do you always make it so hard to dump you and find someone a hundred percent better?! Someone smarter than you. Someone who doesn't burp in church or scratch himself in public.

SECOND ACTOR: Would you rather I scratched in church and burped in public?

FIRST ACTOR: No! I'd rather you just let me beak your heart, shatter your ego, and then move on with my life! Why can't I do that? Huh?!

SECOND ACTOR: I don't know. Maybe because I know just how tight to hold you when you've had a bad day at work. Or how not to get anywhere near you when you're fighting on the phone with your mother. Or maybe it's because I know exactly where to kiss that one... special point on the curve of your neck, that makes your breath gasp and your legs turn into Silly Putty... *(She does so. He melts)*

FIRST ACTOR: Um...uh...what was I saying?

SECOND ACTOR: The usual. But I forgive you...

72.

FIRST ACTOR: Are you okay?

SECOND ACTOR: Yeah.

FIRST ACTOR: I came over as soon as I heard.

SECOND ACTOR: I…uh, I appreciate that.

FIRST ACTOR: Is there anything I can do.

SECOND ACTOR: Haven't you done enough already?

FIRST ACTOR: What do you mean by that? *(No reply)* Look, you know I would never do anything to hurt you.

SECOND ACTOR: That's what I used to think.

FIRST ACTOR: It's true.

SECOND ACTOR: Whatever. Just please stop your lying. I'm not that stupid. I know all about what you did. Every disgusting detail. I even know why you did it.

FIRST ACTOR: It had nothing to do with you.

SECOND ACTOR: Of course not. I probably never even crossed your mind. But don't tell me you'd never hurt me. Because you did more than that. You tore my heart right out of my chest. I trusted you, and you tore my heart out and then stepped all over it.

FIRST ACTOR: I…I'm sorry.

SECOND ACTOR: Well, doesn't that make everything all clean and shiny? You've said your piece. Now it's time for you to go.

FIRST ACTOR: Let me make it up to you…Maybe I can…

SECOND ACTOR: Leave me alone. Please…just get out of here.

FIRST ACTOR: Okay. If that's what you want.

SECOND ACTOR: That's what I want.

FIRST ACTOR: I…I'm sorry.

SECOND ACTOR: Everyone is, sooner or later…

73.

FIRST ACTOR: What's wrong with me?

SECOND ACTOR: What do you mean? There's nothing wrong with you.

FIRST ACTOR: Yes, there is. I'm not as cute or smart or funny as the popular kids. I don't get invited to all the parties. I'm practically invisible to them.

SECOND ACTOR: So maybe they are the ones with the problem. Maybe there's something wrong with them.

FIRST ACTOR: Yeah. Being too popular. That's a big problem. Having lots of friends. How can they stand it?

SECOND ACTOR: You have friends.

FIRST ACTOR: Name five.

SECOND ACTOR: Well, uh… You have me.

FIRST ACTOR: Yeah. We're a two-person popularity parade.

SECOND ACTOR: Maybe what's wrong with you is that you want to be like everyone else, instead of being like yourself.

FIRST ACTOR: Maybe.

SECOND ACTOR: I mean, take away all that flash and cash and good looks and expensive clothes… all those parties and popularity, and what do you have?

FIRST ACTOR: Us.

SECOND ACTOR: You're right. Maybe there's something wrong with us…

74.

FIRST ACTOR: All packed up?

SECOND ACTOR: I guess.

FIRST ACTOR: You don't sound very happy about it. What's the matter? Are you changing your mind?

SECOND ACTOR: No.

FIRST ACTOR: You sure?

SECOND ACTOR: No.

FIRST ACTOR: Come on. This is going to be a good thing.

SECOND ACTOR: Yeah, right.

FIRST ACTOR: We talked about this. You need this. It's the best place for you.

SECOND ACTOR: Uh-huh.

FIRST ACTOR: They can help you there. No more throwing up. No more addictions. No more trouble with the police.

SECOND ACTOR: And if it doesn't work?

FIRST ACTOR: Then we try again. As many times as it takes.

SECOND ACTOR: Why?

FIRST ACTOR: Why? Because I love you. I love you and there's no way I'm going to give up on you. Now move your butt. We need to check in by five.

SECOND ACTOR: I...I'm not sure if I can do this.

FIRST ACTOR: Sure, you can. You can, and you will. And I'll be there with you every step of the way. Got it?

SECOND ACTOR: Got it.

FIRST ACTOR: Okay. Let's go.

75.

FIRST ACTOR: Did you clean up your room?

SECOND ACTOR: I'll do it later.

FIRST ACTOR: I want you to do it now. I said I want you to do it now!

SECOND ACTOR: I heard you.

FIRST ACTOR: You heard me, but for some reason, you didn't feel it necessary to respond? Is that it? I asked you a question, young lady!

SECOND ACTOR: Why are you always yelling at me? I'm not deaf.

FIRST ACTOR: I yell because you are always ignoring me. It's the only way I can get your attention these days. You think I like to yell?

SECOND ACTOR: *(Under her breath.)* Yeah.

FIRST ACTOR: What did you say?

SECOND ACTOR: *(Shouting)* I said 'yeah'. I think you like to yell! That's all you ever do. That's the only way you talk to people these days! You're either yelling or screaming or crying. That's all you ever do.

FIRST ACTOR: Don't you talk to me like that! I'm your mother. I'm all you have left. *(No answer)* Did you hear me?

SECOND ACTOR: Yes, I get it! You're all I have left. Dad died and now you're all I have left… *(Starting to cry)*. But Daddy never yelled at me like this. Dad never… He never…

FIRST ACTOR: I'm sorry, sweetheart. I miss him, too. I miss him so much. *(Softly)* It's okay. We'll be okay… We just have to figure out how to talk to each other again…

Comedic Scenes

76.

FIRST ACTOR: I'm going to kill them!

SECOND ACTOR: You can't.

FIRST ACTOR: Who says I can't?

SECOND ACTOR: Well, the police. Every law on the books. Basic morality and I'm pretty sure the Bible has, "Thou Shalt Not Kill Your Kids" somewhere in there.

FIRST ACTOR: Yeah. But the people who wrote the Bible never met my kids. They would have changed their minds.

SECOND ACTOR: What did they do this time?

FIRST ACTOR: Freddy wet the bed.

SECOND ACTOR: That's not unusual. He's four. Accidents happen.

FIRST ACTOR: This was no accident. He used the garden hose. Fished it through my bedroom window. Flooded the floor, and now my foam mattress is a room-sized sponge. And then Brittney stayed out all night with Teddy.

SECOND ACTOR: Isn't she in preschool?

FIRST ACTOR: Uh huh, and Teddy is an invisible bear, who evidently likes two A.M. tea parties in the camping section of Target. The store's employees have me on speed dial. On top of that, she charged sixty-three dollars in Uber fares to my credit cards to get there. And my nine year-old sold our TV and dining room furniture on Craig's List, so he could buy more Legos. We have to eat at a table made of Legos now!

SECOND ACTOR: What does their father say?

FIRST ACTOR: He hasn't been coherent since they put a spycam in the bathroom. His last bout of constipation is a top-rated YouTube video. Two million hits so far. Wherever he goes, people point and giggle. Maybe if I had a night off... Hey, would you babysit for me this week?

SECOND ACTOR: Nope. No way. Never gonna happen.

77.

FIRST ACTOR: Okay. Here's how it's gonna go. We hit the door at exactly twelve o'clock, Franky and Spike proceed to the two teller's windows, while Fat Wally disarms the guard. And I...

SECOND ACTOR: Excuse me? Can I ask a question?

FIRST ACTOR: What?

SECOND ACTOR: I said 'excuse me. Can I ask a question?'

FIRST ACTOR: I heard what you said. And I said 'what?'

SECOND ACTOR: What do you mean, 'what?'

FIRST ACTOR: What! As in, What the hell is your question?!

SECOND ACTOR: Oh, I see. AM or PM?

FIRST ACTOR: What?

SECOND ACTOR: What, what? I just asked my question. Twelve AM or Twelve PM?

FIRST ACTOR: What kind of question is that?

SECOND ACTOR: Chronological, I think.

FIRST ACTOR: We're holding up a bank. How many banks you know are open at midnight?!

SECOND ACTOR: Counting ATMs and drive-throughs?

FIRST ACTOR: *(Sighs)* You're Earlobe Ernie's kid brother, aren't you?

SECOND ACTOR: That's right. He said to make sure I told you all 'hi!' And that prison isn't all that bad, once you get used to the communal showers, snoring cellmates and cold steel toilet in the middle of your cell.

FIRST ACTOR: *(Annoyed)* I'll keep that in mind... *Moving on*... We hit the front door at precisely twelve. Twelve *noon*...then Franky and Spike proceed to the two teller's windows, while Fat Wally disarms the guard, and then I...

SECOND ACTOR: Uh...excuse me?!

FIRST ACTOR: What is it now?!
SECOND ACTOR: Can I ask one more question?
FIRST ACTOR: *(Growling)* This better be good…
SECOND ACTOR: Look. There's no need to get all grumpy and menacing about it. Just because we are all hardened criminals, doesn't mean we have to be impolite to each other…
FIRST ACTOR: Just ask the damn question!
SECOND ACTOR: Okay. Noon…is that Twelve AM or Twelve PM? I've always get real confused about that. I mean, it's almost morning, so it should be AM…but PM sounds more like midnight to me, since it's all dark and spooky outside, and…
FIRST ACTOR: Will somebody please shoot this guy?!
SECOND ACTOR: Never mind. AM…PM… It's not a big deal. *(Nervously)* Now, where were we?

78.

FIRST ACTOR: I can't stop thinking about you.
SECOND ACTOR: What else is there to think about?
FIRST ACTOR: I'm serious. You're always on my mind. Invading my thoughts. Day and night. Night and day. I think I'm obsessed with you.
SECOND ACTOR: Poor baby.
FIRST ACTOR: And you probably don't think about me at all, do you?
SECOND ACTOR: Of course, I do. Just the other day, I was telling someone how you and I met. How…um, funny you are, and, uh, all about what you do and everything.
FIRST ACTOR: You don't even remember my name, do you?
SECOND ACTOR: Names are so overrated, don't you think?

79.

FIRST ACTOR: What did I do wrong?

SECOND ACTOR: Do you really want to know?

FIRST ACTOR: Yes.

SECOND ACTOR: Well, the outside of the chicken looks like you marinated it in concrete, while the inside is still salmonella pink and dangerous. I assume the clump that resembles volcanic ash used to be some kind of vegetable. And I'm pretty sure mashed potatoes aren't supposed to be that shade of cadaver gray.

FIRST ACTOR: Are you saying I'm a bad cook?

SECOND ACTOR: No. Jeffrey Dahmer was a bad cook. You are Typhoid Mary in the kitchen.

FIRST ACTOR: That's harsh.

SECOND ACTOR: I know. I'm sorry. It's just that after the last three dinner party disasters, I'm getting kind of tired driving our guests to the Emergency Room to have their stomachs pumped. We are running out of friends you haven't accidentally poisoned.

FIRST ACTOR: Most of them recover in a few days!

SECOND ACTOR: I'm not sure that's the true measure of a successful dinner party.

FIRST ACTOR: Can I help it if the stove hates me?

SECOND ACTOR: The stove doesn't hate you. It just hates what you make come out of it. So why don't we do our few remaining friends a favor and pick up some KFC tonight?

FIRST ACTOR: But what do I do with all this food?

SECOND ACTOR: I'm thinking last rites and landfills. As long as the Environmental Protection Agency doesn't catch us.

FIRST ACTOR: Harsh. Really, really harsh.

80.

FIRST ACTOR: Are you still on the computer? It's almost three in the morning.

SECOND ACTOR: There's breaking news out of Togoland. And they just came out with a new herbal Viagra supplement that also cures halitosis and male pattern baldness.

FIRST ACTOR: And none of that can wait 'til tomorrow?

SECOND ACTOR: Hellooo? Don't you care about floppy, hairless guys with bad breath in West Africa?

FIRST ACTOR: No. I care about you falling asleep at work again tomorrow because you're an Internet addict.

SECOND ACTOR: I'm not an Internet addict. I just like staying on top of things. Like politics. The stock market. World religions and current events... Oooh! New celebrity dating scandal! Gotta read this...

FIRST ACTOR: You're hopeless. *(Yawns)* I'm going back to bed.

SECOND ACTOR: Then I guess you'll miss these latest dating, diet and Danish dancing tips...

FIRST ACTOR: Not interested.

SECOND ACTOR: And these secret paparazzi shots of your favorite movie man crush on the French Riviera...

FIRST ACTOR: *(Hesitates)* Skimpy bathing suit?

SECOND ACTOR: You can tell what he was thinking last week.

FIRST ACTOR: I hate you. *(Sits)* Move over. And no more than six levels of Angry Birds tonight.

SECOND ACTOR: Or twelve.

FIRST ACTOR: Okay, twelve. Gosh, he's gorgeous.

SECOND ACTOR: Those six-pack abs are Photoshopped.

FIRST ACTOR: Why can't you be Photoshopped?

81.

FIRST ACTOR: Fancy meeting you here.

SECOND ACTOR: Nothing fancy about this place. That's why I like it. I suppose you're gonna sit down?

FIRST ACTOR: I suppose I am. *(Sits)* I didn't take it, by the way.

SECOND ACTOR: Didn't take what?

FIRST ACTOR: The money.

SECOND ACTOR: I didn't say you did.

FIRST ACTOR: No. But you think I did. I can see it in your eyes.

SECOND ACTOR: Those are bourbon tracks, baby. And for your information, eyes don't talk. Mouths do.

FIRST ACTOR: Except yours. I'm sure nothing even remotely useful ever comes out of your mouth.

SECOND ACTOR: It's an art form. I practiced for years to be this obtuse.

FIRST ACTOR: Obtuse? Well, aren't we the college graduate?

SECOND ACTOR: Not me. Junior High was tough enough. So, let's just say you did take the money...

FIRST ACTOR: Which I didn't.

SECOND ACTOR: Seems only my bloodshot eyes think you did. But assuming they're right...

FIRST ACTOR: Which they're not.

SECOND ACTOR: Hey, they're eyes. Not IQs.

FIRST ACTOR: Funny. How long you been saving that one up?

SECOND ACTOR: About six months. Which is close to the time you opened that secret bank account in the Cayman Islands. Under the name Penelope Streeter, I believe.

FIRST ACTOR: Oh, you're good.

SECOND ACTOR: And you're not. Didn't anyone ever tell you it's not nice to take other people's stuff?

FIRST ACTOR: Just my dad. He was a big time Wall Street banker. But after they put him away for some big-time embezzling, all those cute little daddy lessons took on a somewhat ironic twist. So, what do we do now?

SECOND ACTOR: I dunno. I'm rather enjoying this conversation.

FIRST ACTOR: Me, too.

SECOND ACTOR: But that whole 'Penelope Streeter' thing might make things a little awkward.

FIRST ACTOR: Penelope can do that. What do you say we leave her in the Cayman Islands? Then you and me can go make some more little bourbon tracks on your eyeballs.

SECOND ACTOR: You buying?

FIRST ACTOR: Sorry. All my funds are tied up at the moment.

SECOND ACTOR: That's okay. I know where to find them. And this Penelope. I bet she can really rock a bikini down there in the Caribbean.

FIRST ACTOR: You have no idea.

82.

FIRST ACTOR: It's beautiful here.

SECOND ACTOR: Yup.

FIRST ACTOR: The sun. The sand. The turquoise waves…

SECOND ACTOR: The Pina Coladas. The Mai Tais. The micro-bikini clad hostesses.

FIRST ACTOR: Why do you do that?

SECOND ACTOR: Do what?

FIRST ACTOR: Reduce paradise to a red neck wet dream?

SECOND ACTOR: You have your paradise. I have mine. How about another zombie?

FIRST ACTOR: Might as well.

83.

(First Actor pulls off his shirt. Second Actor covers her mouth)

FIRST ACTOR: What are you doing?!!

SECOND ACTOR: Uh. Nothing. Sorry.

FIRST ACTOR: You were laughing at me!

SECOND ACTOR: No, I wasn't.

FIRST ACTOR: Giggling then.

SECOND ACTOR: Well yeah... I kind of was. But I'm better now. Please continue undressing.

FIRST ACTOR: Are you crazy?

SECOND ACTOR: Do you really need a copy of my psych evaluation?

FIRST ACTOR: What? Of course not. I just wanted to know...Wait. You have a psych evaluation?

SECOND ACTOR: Don't change the subject. Just get back to taking off your clothes.

FIRST ACTOR: *(Drops his pants)* You're giggling again!

SECOND ACTOR: No, I'm not!

FIRST ACTOR: Laughing then.

SECOND ACTOR: I can't help it. How old are you anyway?

FIRST ACTOR: Old enough to do this. Old enough not to like you doing that while I'm doing this!

SECOND ACTOR: I wouldn't be doing this, if you hadn't done that.

FIRST ACTOR: Done what?

SECOND ACTOR: Wrote your name on every piece of your clothes! Even your underwear. What are you? Eight years old and going on your first sleepover?

FIRST ACTOR: Huh? My name isn't on my...? *(Checks his underwear)* Really, Mom?

SECOND ACTOR: *(Giggling again)* Your Mom wrote your name in your clothes? Sorry. Let me try that again without the falsetto. *(Much lower voice)* Your Mom wrote your name in your clothes?

FIRST ACTOR: She called me all upset. A pipe burst in her basement this morning, and I rushed over to fix it.

SECOND ACTOR: And she wrote your name in your clothes as a reward? Man, plumbers have been getting overpaid for years.

FIRST ACTOR: Very funny. I got filthy, and Mom said she'd throw these in the wash for me. She must have written my name in while doing the laundry.

SECOND ACTOR: That is such a Mom thing to do.

FIRST ACTOR: Old habits die hard, I guess. You can stop laughing now. Or giggling. Either one.

SECOND ACTOR: Unlikely.

FIRST ACTOR: Um, I'm guessing this isn't going to happen tonight.

SECOND ACTOR: Even more unlikely. But there is one good thing that came out of this…

FIRST ACTOR: That would be?

SECOND ACTOR: *(Looking inside his waistband)* At least I know you used your real name when you married me.

FIRST ACTOR: Maybe I shouldn't have.

SECOND ACTOR: Oh, my poor baby… You poor widdle man…

FIRST ACTOR: Well, that just killed the mood…

84.

FIRST ACTOR: It's time to get up. Come on. It's time to get up. You need to get a move on!

SECOND ACTOR: Can't. Early morning inertia. I'm pinned to the bed.

FIRST ACTOR: You can't sleep your life away.

SECOND ACTOR: Actually, as far as career choices go, that doesn't sound half bad.

FIRST ACTOR: But this is your big day! Everything is riding on this! Your whole future!

SECOND ACTOR: All the more reason to kiss the pillow for another hour or two…

FIRST ACTOR: Don't you want this?

SECOND ACTOR: What? Caffeine-fueled paranoia over a six-day workweek? Watching numbers on a screen eat up more and more of my life each day? Ulcers at thirty. Gray hair at forty. Stroke at fifty. And if I'm real lucky, I'll have squirreled away enough to pay for my own funeral four days before retirement. Yeah…What's not to want?

FIRST ACTOR: Oh, so you'd rather be living with your parents at forty, dumpster diving at fifty, and be mummified in the National Slacker Museum after you die.

SECOND ACTOR: That's the game plan. I'm dedicating my whole life to being non-committal. Not do anything but give it a hundred-and-ten percent.

FIRST ACTOR: I give up…

SECOND ACTOR: See? Now that's what I'm talking about. Do me a favor and kill the lights on your way out.

85.

FIRST ACTOR: I've been watching you.

SECOND ACTOR: How comforting. Stalk much?

FIRST ACTOR: In a good way. I noticed not one person has been able to talk to you for more than three minutes. A few have tried, but they left in a hurry. Ran for the hills.

SECOND ACTOR: And that doesn't scare you off?

FIRST ACTOR: Actually, I like the challenge.

SECOND ACTOR: A sport dater, huh? It's not about me, or even the hope of a relationship. It's the challenge. The chase. The game. Alpha males on the prowl. I'm almost impressed.

FIRST ACTOR: You got me all wrong. Others may be like that, but I...

SECOND ACTOR: Look...Why don't we just tell all our lies up front and get them out of the way. Then we can attempt to have a real conversation afterwards. Okay?

FIRST ACTOR: Fair enough. *(With feigned sincerity)* I'm an amateur proctologist, and sole heir to the throne of Sweden. I'm four inches taller than I look, much younger than I appear, and far wiser than I ever imagined I'd ever be. I'm listed in the Guinness Book of World Records for stationary bungee jumping, and won an Oscar last year for best teeth in a dramatic feature film. I play cribbage every Saturday morning with Warren Buffett, Jennifer Lawrence and the Pope, who has sometimes been known to miscount points. I purchased a small Latin American country, but only get to visit it occasionally. Many of my body parts are patent pending. I'm working on the Great American Novel, but it's not finished yet, because I'm writing it in five languages at once, and those Chinese picture-letters can be a real bitch. In my free time, I darn my own socks, design US currency, and knit my own trash bags. *(smiles)* Now you lie to me.

SECOND ACTOR: Okay... I think you have a wonderful sense of humor...

86.

FIRST ACTOR: Aww. Look how cute they are!

SECOND ACTOR: Yeah. Out in the park. Playing with their toys.

FIRST ACTOR: It always amazes me what they can do at that age.

SECOND ACTOR: It's adorable. It really is.

FIRST ACTOR: I know. You spend months and months trying to teach them. Going through the same thing, over and over again. Then suddenly, it's like they just get it. And pretty soon, there they are, doing it all by themselves!

SECOND ACTOR: I know. Last week my Mom couldn't even find the volume control on her phone. Now look at her. She's downloading her own ringtones!

FIRST ACTOR: Sounds like some oldies hit. She's even dancing to it. Uh, if you call that dancing.

SECOND ACTOR: And look at your Dad with his iPad. How cute is that?

FIRST ACTOR: He still can't figure out Twitter, and has absolutely no idea how to SnapChat …but at least he's playing Words With Friends with my aunts.

SECOND ACTOR: It's a start.

FIRST ACTOR: Uh oh. He has that blank look on his face again.

SECOND ACTOR: That's never a good sign.

FIRST ACTOR: I know. I better go help him. *(Calling out)* Just hit the home button, Dad, The home button! *(Pause)* No! Not with a stick!

87.

FIRST ACTOR: Can I help you?
SECOND ACTOR: No. Maybe. Can you tell me where the break room is?
FIRST ACTOR: The break room is for employees only.
SECOND ACTOR: I know. And man, do I need a break.
FIRST ACTOR: You mean, you work here?
SECOND ACTOR: Uh-huh. I do get paychecks. So, yeah. I guess I do.
FIRST ACTOR: That's funny. I've never seen you around before. Are you new here?
SECOND ACTOR: Not really. I've worked here for a while now.
FIRST ACTOR: You have?
SECOND ACTOR: Uh huh. Ten years. The office down the hall from you.
FIRST ACTOR: The big corner office? The one that always has a 'Do Not Disturb' sign on it?
SECOND ACTOR: I like my privacy.
FIRST ACTOR: Privacy? This is the Department of Motor Vehicles!
SECOND ACTOR: So that's why all these people are standing around waiting in lines?
FIRST ACTOR: You didn't know?
SECOND ACTOR: Actually, I work at home a lot.
FIRST ACTOR: What can you do out of your home for the Department of Motor Vehicles?
SECOND ACTOR: I'm not really sure. I'm still reading through my job requirements.
FIRST ACTOR: But you've been working here ten years!
SECOND ACTOR: That's right. And I'm up for a raise soon.
FIRST ACTOR: You're related to someone in politics, aren't you?
SECOND ACTOR: How did you know?

88.

FIRST ACTOR: Can I tell you something?

SECOND ACTOR: Shhh! Keep your voice down…

FIRST ACTOR: *(Whispering)* I don't think we should be doing this.

SECOND ACTOR: Why not?

FIRST ACTOR: It's wrong. And couldn't we get in real trouble for this?

SECOND ACTOR: Of course, we can. It's a criminal act.

FIRST ACTOR: But we're not criminals.

SECOND ACTOR: Du-uh. If we are performing a criminal act, then it follows that we are, indeed, criminals. That's Logic 101.

FIRST ACTOR: What if we get caught?

SECOND ACTOR: I suggest we don't.

FIRST ACTOR: But what if we do?

SECOND ACTOR: Then we get caught. We go to jail. And you get to share a cell with real criminals. The kind that don't get second thoughts before they commit an act of vandalism.

FIRST ACTOR: Are you serious?

SECOND ACTOR: Only partially. Are you getting cold feet?

FIRST ACTOR: I'm getting cold everything! It's freezing out here.

SECOND ACTOR: Life in the fast lane. Are we gonna do this, or what? *(No reply)* I said, are we gonna do this, or what?!

FIRST ACTOR: *(Pause)* Okay. Give me the toilet paper.

SECOND ACTOR: You take these three rolls and toss them up into those trees. I'll TP her car and front porch. That'll teach Gail Wynslinger to break up with you by text message!

FIRST ACTOR: I guess.

89.

FIRST ACTOR: Ugh. What could be worse than housework?!

SECOND ACTOR: Let me see. War. Plague. Famine. Sitcom Reruns.

FIRST ACTOR: You know what I mean. I vacuum this floor three times a day. And do at least six thousand loads of laundry a week.

SECOND ACTOR: You don't think that might be a slight exaggeration?

FIRST ACTOR: Not at all. I live with barnyard animals who refuse to pick up their underwear!

SECOND ACTOR: Do barnyard animals even wear underwear?

FIRST ACTOR: Civilized ones do. I live with the barely civilized ones. Offer me a domesticated donkey and a castrated goat, and I'll trade in the kids any day.

SECOND ACTOR: You don't mean that. You love the kids.

FIRST ACTOR: So I'll visit them once or twice a month. In the barn.

SECOND ACTOR: You're just tired. What can I do to help?

FIRST ACTOR: Wash the dishes. Pick up your mess. Take out the trash.

SECOND ACTOR: I meant something without effort.

FIRST ACTOR: This relationship isn't working out.

SECOND ACTOR: It is for me. I get someone to do the laundry. Vacuum the floor. Wash the dishes. Pick up my…

FIRST ACTOR: I am *this close* to strangling you with the vacuum hose.

SECOND ACTOR: Okay. You're right. You are amazing, and I do take you for granted. Starting tomorrow, I want you to give me a big long list of chores, and I'll do every one of them.

FIRST ACTOR: I thought you were going out of town tomorrow?

SECOND ACTOR: Oh, that's right… Must have slipped my mind.

FIRST ACTOR: Where's that vacuum cleaner hose?! Where is it?!

90.

FIRST ACTOR: Okay. I've decided what I'm going to be in life.

SECOND ACTOR: And what's that?

FIRST ACTOR: I'm going to be…exceptional!

SECOND ACTOR: You're going to be exceptional?

FIRST ACTOR: That's right.

SECOND ACTOR: At what?

FIRST ACTOR: What do you mean 'at what?' At everything.

SECOND ACTOR: You are going to exceptional at everything?

FIRST ACTOR: Impressively so. Anyway, that's my plan.

SECOND ACTOR: It's not easy to be exceptional at everything. Most people can't be exceptional at anything at all.

FIRST ACTOR: I'm not most people.

SECOND ACTOR: Right…. But don't you think you should focus a little? Choose one thing that you're good at?

FIRST ACTOR: Aargh! You don't get it all…I don't want to be good at just one thing…I don't even want to be good at a *lot of things*…I plan to be *exceptional* at *everything!*

SECOND ACTOR: Like painting and soccer?

FIRST ACTOR: Uh-huh.

SECOND ACTOR: Cooking and chemistry.

FIRST ACTOR: Exceptional at both.

SECOND ACTOR: Typing and tap dancing. Singing and sky-diving. Rock climbing and rock music.

FIRST ACTOR: Exceptional… Exceptional… And Exceptional.

SECOND ACTOR: Farming and physics. Calculus and construction work. Bowling and brain surgery.

FIRST ACTOR: Now you got it. I'll be exceptional at everything!

SECOND ACTOR: You know, that's not a bad plan. Maybe I should be exceptional, too?

FIRST ACTOR: Exceptional at what?

SECOND ACTOR: At everything.

FIRST ACTOR: Sorry. That's my gig. Maybe you should try being…I don't know…above average at something first?

91.

FIRST ACTOR: I just don't get it. How can we not know where something is? Only where it's not?

SECOND ACTOR: That's Heisenberg's Uncertainty Principle. On the atomic scale, the very act of seeing something interferes with where it should be.

FIRST ACTOR: Are you making this up?

SECOND ACTOR: No. It's modern physics. Quantum mechanics, actually. You can only see where something was, and by the time you see it, it's not there anymore.

FIRST ACTOR: I don't get it…

SECOND ACTOR: Even the light you shine at something may affect its position…if it's smaller than the photons or wave particles that bounce off it, enabling you to see it in the first place. Therefore, it moves, and you only know where it's not.

FIRST ACTOR: Heisenberg's Uncertainty Principle, huh?

SECOND ACTOR: That's right. Bottom line, nothing is ultimately knowable.

FIRST ACTOR: And that's your excuse for not remembering where you left your car keys?

SECOND ACTOR: Either that, or I'm just plain stupid.

92.

SECOND ACTOR: Don't eat that!!

FIRST ACTOR: Huh? What? Who are you?!

SECOND ACTOR: I'm your future self, and I'm here to warn you not to eat that pizza!

FIRST ACTOR: My future self? You don't look anything like me.

SECOND ACTOR: Years from now, you've had surgeries. Lots of surgeries. *(Shudders)* But it's okay. Everyone in the future has them. New face. New body. Even a new gender every year. It all gets very confusing.

FIRST ACTOR: Sorry. Not buying it.

SECOND ACTOR: I am your future self. How else would I know about your crush on Miss Geary in the sixth grade? Your fear of dryer lint? That 'special' folder on your computer, and how often you...

FIRST ACTOR: Okay! Enough! Future self. I believe you. So why are you here?

SECOND ACTOR: To stop you from eating that last piece of pizza. You've already had seven, at four hundred and ninety calories each. This is a pivotal moment in your life. That last piece is the one that pushes you over the edge. A few years from now, you'll be three hundred and ninety pounds, with clogged arteries and a digestive tract more clogged than a California freeway.

FIRST ACTOR: *(Shrugs)* I can live with that.

SECOND ACTOR: No, you can't! Right this moment, I'm lying in a hospital bed, waiting for my sixth heart transplant.

FIRST ACTOR: Sixth?

SECOND ACTOR: Baboon heart. And everything from your small intestines to your colon has been replaced by high tech intestinal garden hose.

FIRST ACTOR: Intestinal garden hose?

SECOND ACTOR: Trust me. It ain't pretty.

FIRST ACTOR: So…so what can I do?

SECOND ACTOR: Put down that pizza. Cancel Netflix. And start doing push-ups.

FIRST ACTOR: I do push-ups.

SECOND ACTOR: More than one a month.

FIRST ACTOR: Damn.

SECOND ACTOR: Do it for your health. Do it for me. Do it for Babette.

FIRST ACTOR: Babette?

SECOND ACTOR: Future girlfriend. Grad student. Best part of your nineties.

FIRST ACTOR: Push-ups and no more pizza?

SECOND ACTOR: For Babette. You can do it.

FIRST ACTOR: *(Sighs)* For Babette. *(Puts down the pizza)*

SECOND ACTOR: Thatta boy!

FIRST ACTOR: The future better be worth it…

(First Actor Exits. After a beat, Second Actor dives for the pizza. Swallows it whole)

SECOND ACTOR: Sucker…Ummmm. Delicious…

93.

FIRST ACTOR: Can you help me?

SECOND ACTOR: That depends. What do you need?

FIRST ACTOR: Not much. Worldwide fame and admiration. A winning Powerball ticket. Someone to love me forever.

SECOND ACTOR: Is that all?

FIRST ACTOR: For now. My list gets longer around Christmas.

SECOND ACTOR: I bet. Well, I can't help you with one and two, but number three may be doable.

FIRST ACTOR: Someone to love me forever? Who'd you have in mind?

SECOND ACTOR: Me, actually.

FIRST ACTOR: Hmmmm. I don't know. My standards are pretty high. Do you have a resume of your past relationships? Along with references. Written references.

SECOND ACTOR: Sorry, no references. I'm not usually attracted to women who can read and write.

FIRST ACTOR: Why am I not surprised? Did any of these women know they were actually in a relationship with you? Or did you stalk them from afar?

SECOND ACTOR: You call it stalking, I call it overly excessive uninvited attention. Besides, physical contact and communication can be so intrusive. Most of my old girlfriends preferred a lot of personal space. Sometimes continents.

FIRST ACTOR: You're crazy, you know that?

SECOND ACTOR: But willing to love you forever. If that works for you?

FIRST ACTOR: Let me think about it...So no-go on the Powerball and worldwide fame and admiration?

SECOND ACTOR: Sorry.

FIRST ACTOR: I guess I'll have to make do. Now get on over here and kiss me. Repeatedly, if you don't mind.

94.

FIRST ACTOR: Tell me you didn't!

SECOND ACTOR: Didn't what?

FIRST ACTOR: Don't play innocent with me. Just tell me you didn't do it! Tell me you're smarter than that!

SECOND ACTOR: Well, I could tell you…

FIRST ACTOR: Oh my God… You did, didn't you?

SECOND ACTOR: I don't know what you're talking about.

FIRST ACTOR: Don't give me that. You know exactly what I'm talking about! And I can't believe you would be so…so…

SECOND ACTOR: Calm down. There were extenuating circumstances.

FIRST ACTOR: Extenuating circumstances?! Do you realize how embarrassing this is for me?

SECOND ACTOR: You may be overreacting just a bit…

FIRST ACTOR: Overreacting? Overreacting!! She's my aunt!

SECOND ACTOR: You're point being?

FIRST ACTOR: She's my aunt! A blood relative. People will talk! I'll never be able to show my face in this town again! And we can forget family gatherings at Christmas!

SECOND ACTOR: Hey, you said yourself it was an ugly painting. The absolute worst wedding gift we received. You hate it as much as I did. So, while you were out, I went to the store and exchanged it for something better. Something we wouldn't be embarrassed to have hanging in our house. There's nothing scandalous about that.

FIRST ACTOR: You don't know my aunt.

SECOND ACTOR: Well, we both know her taste…and dancing hippos in pink tutus ain't gonna cut it…

95.

FIRST ACTOR: This is a special night.

SECOND ACTOR: Two adults splitting a Happy Meal is not exactly what I would call 'special.'

FIRST ACTOR: It's not about the food. It's about the company. You and me. Did you ever think we'd make it this far? The two of us, still together?

SECOND ACTOR: No way. We have zero compatibility. We don't even like each other on the sub-atomic scale. And did I mention we are sharing a kid's meal at McDonald's?

FIRST ACTOR: Look at the bright side. Here we are. Celebrating our second anniversary.

SECOND ACTOR: Log in to reality, freak boy. It's only our third date.

FIRST ACTOR: To you, it may be a third date. To me, it's the second anniversary of our first date. It's all a matter of perspective.

SECOND ACTOR: They offer therapy to those with your type of perspective. And drugs. Heavy, heavy drugs.

FIRST ACTOR: Love is the only drug I need. And I'm overdosing on you tonight.

SECOND ACTOR: It's a shame I have no gag reflex, because that line would have triggered it big time.

FIRST ACTOR: Hey, I'm giving you my 'A game' here. I don't squander all this charm on just anybody. You should be flattered.

SECOND ACTOR: And you should be arrested for selling that much cheese without a license. Sorry, but a plastic toy and twelve-and-a-half French fries apiece doesn't scream lasting relationship to me. You'll have to celebrate the second anniversary of our first date without me. *(Exits)*

FIRST ACTOR: I love when they play hard to get. *(Calling after her)* That is what you're doing, right? Playing hard to get? Aren't you? Is that what this is?

96.

FIRST ACTOR: What are you doing watching TV?

SECOND ACTOR: Um, the TV is on and I'm watching it. I'm pretty sure that's how it's supposed to work.

FIRST ACTOR: Don't get smart with me. What about your homework? What's today's excuse?

SECOND ACTOR: No excuse. I finished my homework.

FIRST ACTOR: Great. I'm proud of you. Where is it?

SECOND ACTOR: Well, see, that's the thing... I finished it and put it on the kitchen counter. Only now I can't find it.

FIRST ACTOR: How original. I suppose the dog ate it?

SECOND ACTOR: We don't have a dog. We have a cat. And I already checked the litter box to see if anything familiar came out the other end.

FIRST ACTOR: Why would your homework come out the... Wait a minute... What class was this for?

SECOND ACTOR: Chemistry. The assignment was to make a new type of compost that didn't smell bad. I used some cocoa, and one of your Bath & Body Works candles to make mine smell like chocolate. I put it in that big glass baking pan and left it right there on the counter.

FIRST ACTOR: You put your compost experiment in my glass baking pan? And left it on the kitchen counter?

SECOND ACTOR: I promise! And it was gone when I got up for school this morning. I'm telling the truth! Honest.

FIRST ACTOR: Oh, my God! Dad left a note saying he was taking the pan of brownies to work!

SECOND ACTOR: You don't think he...?

FIRST ACTOR: I have to call him before he feeds his boss chocolate-smelling compost! Oh, my God!

97.

FIRST ACTOR: Happy Valentine's Day.

SECOND ACTOR: As if.

FIRST ACTOR: Let me guess. Single. Alone. All your friends paired up and stupid with love?

SECOND ACTOR: Every one of them. And you?

FIRST ACTOR: Serial divorcee. I made the Guinness Book Of World Records for Dumbest Relationship Choices nine years in a row.

SECOND ACTOR: I hear that. You do the online dating thing yet?

FIRST ACTOR: The instant my last divorce was final. I took the sixteen dollars my ex and the lawyers left me and fell for that whole 'love of my life is waiting online' fantasy. But everyone I met online was even more screwed up than I was.

SECOND ACTOR: At least you had something in common. I had to hang out at the produce counter at the Dizzy Discount Food Mart to find someone who was even close to a possibility. Turned out all we had in common was day-old doughnuts and wilted broccoli.

FIRST ACTOR: You try Tinder? Bumble? OkCupid? PlentyOfFish?

SECOND ACTOR: Uh huh. Crashed and burned every single time. I think even my iPhone was starting to feel sorry for me.

FIRST ACTOR: Being single in the Twenty-First Century really sucks, doesn't it?

SECOND ACTOR: Majorly. I so envy my great-great-great-grandparents. They had an arranged marriage at thirteen years-old.

FIRST ACTOR: But they were happy, right?

SECOND ACTOR: Not even close. He was the town drunk, who lost their life savings betting blacksmiths would never go out of style. And she slammed the door on sex after their fifteenth kid.

FIRST ACTOR: I don't blame her. Still, it must have been a lot easier way back when.

SECOND ACTOR: Yeah. Limited choices. And if you got stuck with someone ugly or stupid, at least you didn't have to live that long. That's a plus.

FIRST ACTOR: Hard life. Grinding poverty. Early death. Practically a fairy tale.

SECOND ACTOR: I have to say, it's good to meet another depressed cynic on Valentine's Day. So, what are you up to tonight?

FIRST ACTOR: What else? Drowning in bourbon and self-pity. And just for fun, I spit these heart-shaped candies at every happy looking couple that walks by.

SECOND ACTOR: The chalky Valentine candies with all the overly cute messages on them? I hate those! They are the ultimate sugary insult to all the lonely people in the world.

FIRST ACTOR: Yeah. Using them as slimy projectiles to terrorize lovebirds is almost metaphorical.

SECOND ACTOR: Pure genius. Give me some.

FIRST ACTOR: Here you go. With the right lip technique and the proper amount of breath, you can splat a pair of lovebirds as they stare lovingly into each other's eyes.

SECOND ACTOR: Give me some.

FIRST ACTOR: Sure. And look...Here come some 'first daters' now. Grab a handful and give it a try.

SECOND ACTOR: Now what?

FIRST ACTOR: Take a deep breath. Pop two in your mouth. Aim for the ears...Got 'em! Great shot! You're a natural!

SECOND ACTOR: Thanks. This is turning out to be a Happy Valentine's Day after all!

98.

FIRST ACTOR: Aaaarrrrgh! Do you have to be a *complete* idiot to run for office?

SECOND ACTOR: No, but it helps.

FIRST ACTOR: This one just lied her way out of yet another scandal and cover up. Her twenty-fourth, I think. That one has a proven track record for screwing up everything he ever touched. And this year's media darling has the brains of a flea and the mouth of a trash-talking preschooler. Did you hear those debates?

SECOND ACTOR: Those aren't debates. It's Animal House. You don't get into the Electoral College unless you're head of a party. I think they should kill the debates altogether and settle it with beer pong.

FIRST ACTOR: Good idea. I can't believe in a country of over a third of a billion people, these jokers are the best we can come up with. I mean, seriously. Are these the finest examples of intelligent and integrity America has to offer?

SECOND ACTOR: Politics is a popularity contest, and we always choose the Class Clown over the Valedictorian. Why do you think celebrity know-nothings make a gajillion dollars more than the average NASA scientist?

FIRST ACTOR: I wonder what those guys who wrote the Constitution would think of this latest crop of candidates?

SECOND ACTOR: I say it's all their fault. They decided it was our God-given inalienable right to vote for bumblers, bozos and brain-dead bureaucrats. The natural devolution of democracy. Why are you making it such a big deal?

FIRST ACTOR: Let me see… War. The economy. Crippling national debt. Random psychopaths shooting up schools and movie theaters. Income inequality and racial hatred. Government corruption. Global warming or cooling, whatever they say it is this week…

SECOND ACTOR: Relax, man. That's why we have Netflix. Just toss in another Adam Sandler movie, and even these guys'll look intelligent.

FIRST ACTOR: Happy Madison's not running for president, is he?

SECOND ACTOR: Hope so. He couldn't be any more of a joke than the last eight years. Hand me the popcorn…

99.

FIRST ACTOR: I can't believe it!

SECOND ACTOR: It's true. We're getting married on the fifteenth.

FIRST ACTOR: But you've only known him three months?

SECOND ACTOR: I know. Everybody thinks we're crazy. But sometimes you just know it.

FIRST ACTOR: Know what? Know his family? Know his secrets? Know what makes him mad? Know how long he stays in a relationship before he starts getting restless? Are those the things you know after only three months?

SECOND ACTOR: You're right. Maybe I don't know any of those things. And yes, maybe we are crazy. But what I do know is that this is the first man who ever listened like he was really interested in what I was saying. The first boyfriend to ever hold me when I needed him to, without asking questions, or trying to fix what was wrong with me. The first guy who ever told me I was beautiful…and made me feel like he really meant it.

FIRST ACTOR: That doesn't mean he'll always…

SECOND ACTOR: He probably won't always…and maybe I won't either. But this is the first time I have ever said 'I love you' to someone…and knew that I meant it with every piece of my soul.

FIRST ACTOR: Well, in that case… Does he have a brother?

100.

FIRST ACTOR: OMG, Melissa! I am soooo sorry!

SECOND ACTOR: I am totally dying of embarrassment here. Do you think everyone knows?

FIRST ACTOR: Uh, yeah! She's telling everyone.

SECOND ACTOR: Kill me now.

FIRST ACTOR: Why did you let her come?

SECOND ACTOR: How could I stop her? The second my mom heard we were having a school dance, she set her giggle to overflow, saying 'I want to chaperone!' I thought my head would explode all over the dinner table.

FIRST ACTOR: Like who needs chaperones anyway? We are in eighth grade. That's practically high school!

SECOND ACTOR: I know, right? But you know my mom. She is so stuck in that 1950s Civil War 'hide your daughters in the barn' era. She wouldn't even let me date until I was 13.

FIRST ACTOR: Wow. That is so Stalin.

SECOND ACTOR: Who's Stalin?

FIRST ACTOR: Some bossy guy. I think he came over on the Mayflower with my grandfather, or something.

SECOND ACTOR: Of course, she has to tell everyone our family secrets.

FIRST ACTOR: I heard her telling all the boys what a catch you are, now that you're no longer in that 'awkward phase.'.

SECOND ACTOR: She said that?!!!

FIRST ACTOR: I think she thinks she's helping. *(Looks up)* Uh oh. Looks like she's showing your baby bathtub pictures to Tommy Everest.

SECOND ACTOR: No! She is soooo not doing that! Not Tommy Everest! He was my third-grade crush!! What's Tommy doing now?!

FIRST ACTOR: Taking a cell phone shot of your baby picture.
SECOND ACTOR: Gag me! He just SnapChatted my own baby bathtub picture back to me!
FIRST ACTOR: Wow. Your toddler tush is going to live online forever.
SECOND ACTOR: Kill me now. *(Yelling)* Not cute, Mom! Not cute!!

101.

FIRST ACTOR: You're cute.
SECOND ACTOR: Can't help it. An accident of birth.
FIRST ACTOR: Funny, too.
SECOND ACTOR: I should have been a comedian. Not the stand-up kind. I'm way too lazy for that.
FIRST ACTOR: Do you have any idea how adorable you are?
SECOND ACTOR: On a scale of one to ten? I'd say somewhere between newborn puppies and baby's first step.... And that's not even on my good days.
FIRST ACTOR: All I can think about is you. Day and night. Just imagining what it would be like holding you close. Closer than you've ever been held before. Wrapping my arms around you. Losing myself in your soft brown eyes. Imagining the warm, tender touch of your lips. Tracing my hungry fingers along your soft cheek, the subtle curve of your neck, to your gently heaving chest. Slowly, surrendering all my inhibitions to the velvety pleading in your voice...
SECOND ACTOR: Uh... Okay. You got my attention. What was your name again?

102.

FIRST ACTOR: Excuse me! You with the face! I said excuse me!

SECOND ACTOR: Huh? Are you talking to me?

FIRST ACTOR: Of course, I'm talking to you. I'm looking in your direction and my lips are moving. That means I'm talking to you, doesn't it?

SECOND ACTOR: I suppose.

FIRST ACTOR: You don't recognize me, do you?

SECOND ACTOR: Sorry, but no.

FIRST ACTOR: I was the person standing behind you in the grocery store just now.

SECOND ACTOR: Oh...kay...

FIRST ACTOR: In the Express Lane. Fifteen Items or Less.

SECOND ACTOR: And?

FIRST ACTOR: And you had sixteen.

SECOND ACTOR: Are you serious?

FIRST ACTOR: Yes, I'm serious. And I can count too! You had sixteen items in a Fifteen Items or Less lane.

SECOND ACTOR: I had eleven.

FIRST ACTOR: You had sixteen. Two bags of chips. A jar of salsa. One chocolate cake and twelve cans of beer. That's sixteen items.

SECOND ACTOR: It was two six-packs of beer. A six-pack counts as one item!

FIRST ACTOR: Not unless you invite me to the party.

SECOND ACTOR: Does that work for you often?

FIRST ACTOR: All the time. You'd be amazed at the number of parties I get invited to. So, what are we celebrating?

103.

FIRST ACTOR: Where have you been?

SECOND ACTOR: Out.

FIRST ACTOR: Out where?

SECOND ACTOR: Out shopping.

FIRST ACTOR: What do you mean, 'out shopping?'

SECOND ACTOR: You want the dictionary definition? Or the step-by-step instructions?

FIRST ACTOR: I thought I took your credit cards away?

SECOND ACTOR: That was you? I went crazy looking for them! You had no right to…

FIRST ACTOR: I have every right! Don't you understand? We are broke. Busted! There's nothing left in the bank accounts. We're cleaned out. And now you go shopping with money we don't have?!

SECOND ACTOR: That's right. I went shopping with money we don't have. I had to borrow money from my mother, just so I could buy food for our children.

FIRST ACTOR: You borrowed money from your mother?

SECOND ACTOR: Yes. *(Sarcastically)* She sends her love, by the way.

FIRST ACTOR: I…I didn't know. I'm sorry.

SECOND ACTOR: Save it. Now if we're finished here, I need to cook dinner before they cut off our electricity.

FIRST ACTOR: Really, I'm sorry, I… *(Suddenly)* Wait a minute… Is that a new purse?

SECOND ACTOR: *(Happily)* Yes. And it was on sale. Just a hundred and eighty-nine dollars! And these shoes were on sale too. And they had the cutest little…

FIRST ACTOR: Aaaaaaaaaarrrgh!

104.

FIRST ACTOR: Hello.

SECOND ACTOR: Hello yourself.

FIRST ACTOR: Nice party.

SECOND ACTOR: It better be. I don't get dressed this fine for nothing.

FIRST ACTOR: I must say, you look hot. Really hot.

SECOND ACTOR: Excuse me…Are you trying to pick me up?

FIRST ACTOR: Would it be a bad thing if I was?

SECOND ACTOR: Well, considering this is my wedding…

FIRST ACTOR: That's makes it a little more exciting, don't you think?

SECOND ACTOR: I do.

FIRST ACTOR: You already said that to me once today.

SECOND ACTOR: Promise me you still intend to flirt with me like this, even after we've been married forty years.

FIRST ACTOR: I do.

105.

FIRST ACTOR: Tell me something. Do you enjoy being like this?

SECOND ACTOR: Being like what?

FIRST ACTOR: So unsure of yourself.

SECOND ACTOR: What? I'm not unsure of myself?

FIRST ACTOR: Are you sure?

SECOND ACTOR: I think so. I mean yes. Of course, I'm sure. I am sure that I'm sure of myself.

FIRST ACTOR: Doesn't sound like it to me. I've seen hamsters with more self-esteem.

SECOND ACTOR: What are you talking about? I'm a big success. Well off. Drive a Maserati convertible. Top of the line.

FIRST ACTOR:	Over-compensating. How sad.
SECOND ACTOR:	I'm not over-compensating!
FIRST ACTOR:	Are you sure?
SECOND ACTOR:	Yes, I'm sure! I've got absolutely nothing to over-compensate for!
FIRST ACTOR:	They say that's the first sign…

106.

FIRST ACTOR:	Don't ever let me do that again!
SECOND ACTOR:	As if I could have stopped you.
FIRST ACTOR:	You could have. You could have warned me that Midol, mimosas and marijuana don't mix. Or that there really isn't such a thing as nude karaoke.
SECOND ACTOR:	Especially at your kid's PTA meeting.
FIRST ACTOR:	He's only in kindergarten, and I pretty sure I've scarred him for life!
SECOND ACTOR:	Only emotionally. Looks like the cafeteria lady was physically scarred. That food fight was close to an Olympic event.
FIRST ACTOR:	I probably should send her flowers. Maybe when she comes out of the coma.
SECOND ACTOR:	*(Checking cell phone)* Oh, look. Somebody's already posted the video on Facebook.
FIRST ACTOR:	Oh, my God! I'll never be able to show my face in this town again!
SECOND ACTOR:	That's not your face that's showing…
FIRST ACTOR:	Oh, my God!

107.

FIRST ACTOR: Okay, listen up. We can't let these poser thugs step off into our turf and think they can just squeeze us out. We gotta show 'em we don't fall easy. You feel me?

SECOND ACTOR: I would never do that.

FIRST ACTOR: Do what?

SECOND ACTOR: Feel you. I mean, we're friends and all, but…

FIRST ACTOR: It's an expression. It's street. It means you understand what I'm saying.

SECOND ACTOR: Sorry. I'm from the suburbs. Still trying to learn the vernacular.

FIRST ACTOR: Then stop using words like 'vernacular.' It's hard to prove you're hardcore, when you say things like 'vernacular.' Feel me?

SECOND ACTOR: No, I would nev…oh, um, yeah. I am feeling you a lot.

FIRST ACTOR: Close enough. Like I was sayin', we head on down to Fourth Street, kick in their door, and…

SECOND ACTOR: Will we have guns?

FIRST ACTOR: Hell, no. Whatta you think we are? Criminals?

SECOND ACTOR: Well, if we kick in their door, that is somewhat criminal-ish behavior…

FIRST ACTOR: No guns. We just kick in their door and…

SECOND ACTOR: What if they have guns?

FIRST ACTOR: Huh?

SECOND ACTOR: What if we go down there all gangsta-like, kick in their door without any guns, but then find out that they have their own guns?

FIRST ACTOR: I don't think so.

SECOND ACTOR: But what if they do? And since they will probably be really really mad that we damaged their doorway, what if they decide to point their guns all gangsta-like at us?

FIRST ACTOR: Then we run. It's not like any of us are lookin' to catch a bullet or something.

SECOND ACTOR: I don't know. Running doesn't seem all that hardcore to me. I mean, I like the kicking in the door stuff and all, but the running away part seems a bit anti-climactic.

FIRST ACTOR: Dude, you ever see Scarface? Straight Outta Compton? Purge Anarchy? You ever hear even one of those ice-cold killers say things were getting 'a bit anti-climactic?'

SECOND ACTOR: I haven't seen any of them. My mom has a Parental Block on our Netflix subscription.

FIRST ACTOR: You're killing me.

SECOND ACTOR: Is that like I'm feeling you? Do I kill you first, then feel you? Or am I supposed to feel you first, then kill you? I just want to get it right...

FIRST ACTOR: Why did you even join this gang?

SECOND ACTOR: My mom said I was playing too many video games. She said I should go out and make some new friends.

FIRST ACTOR: *(Sighs)* Just shoot me...

SECOND ACTOR: I can't. We don't have any guns. I can feel you though. Would that help?

108.

FIRST ACTOR: *(SFX: Phone)* Phone's ringing! *(SFX: Phone)* I said the phone's ringing!

SECOND ACTOR: I know.

FIRST ACTOR: Then why don't you answer it?

SECOND ACTOR: It's not for me.

FIRST ACTOR: How do you know? *(Picks up phone)* Hello? Hello? Dammit, they hung up! You are so…irresponsible!

SECOND ACTOR: They'll call back.

FIRST ACTOR: How do you know? You don't even know who it was!

SECOND ACTOR: It's 9:45 AM. That means it was your boss trying to find out why you are late again, and what stupid excuse you are going to make up this time. He'll figure you dodged his first call, and then call back again in exactly… *(SFX: Phone)* … now.

FIRST ACTOR: Don't answer it!!

109.

FIRST ACTOR: Will it ever stop snowing?!!

SECOND ACTOR: Probably sometime around August.

FIRST ACTOR: This has been the worst winter! How weird is it that I could actually be warmer inside my refrigerator?

SECOND ACTOR: Leftovers don't know how lucky they are.

FIRST ACTOR: No kidding. I have three pair of socks on, and my toes still feel like miniature popsicles.

SECOND ACTOR: Can you imagine how bad it would be if we actually went outside?

FIRST ACTOR: Man was never meant to live like this! Woman wasn't meant to live like this! I don't even think polar bears were meant to live like this!

SECOND ACTOR: I think that's an exaggeration.

FIRST ACTOR: Nuh-unh. I'm way too cold to exaggerate. Do you hear that sound?

SECOND ACTOR: What sound?

FIRST ACTOR: The sound of my ribs chattering. Or maybe it's my liver.

SECOND ACTOR: Okay, then how about if I just move a little closer? You know, we could snuggle up and share some body heat. Purely for survival reasons.

FIRST ACTOR: Share body heat with you? Uh, no thanks. I'm pretty sure I'd rather freeze.

SECOND ACTOR: You are such a cold person, you know it?

FIRST ACTOR: Could I make it any more obvious?

110.

FIRST ACTOR: We're heading out to Mangini's after work. Free appetizers during Happy Hour. Want to come?

SECOND ACTOR: Thanks, but I'm on a food-free diet.

FIRST ACTOR: A food-free diet? What's that?

SECOND ACTOR: You drink two gallons of water and lemon juice, then pee thirty times a day.

FIRST ACTOR: Uh, sounds great. How long have you been on it?

SECOND ACTOR: What day is this?

FIRST ACTOR: Friday.

SECOND ACTOR: Let me see… one…three…about four and a half hours so far. I'm so hungry, I drool on my laptop every time a pizza ad pops up.

FIRST ACTOR: Peeing and drooling. God, I hate bikini season.

SECOND ACTOR: Guys don't know how easy they have it.

111.

FIRST ACTOR: BigBugBigBugBigBugBigBugBigBug!

SECOND ACTOR: What is it? A spider?

FIRST ACTOR: Too big to be a spider. More like a raccoon. Or a coyote. A big black coyote. With eight legs.

SECOND ACTOR: You're exaggerating.

FIRST ACTOR: I'm not exaggerating! It's like something out of those cheap 1950's horror flicks. Where insects grow ginormous from a megadose of nuclear waste.

SECOND ACTOR: That must be it. They must have installed a leaky nuclear reactor down the street while we were sleeping. *(Sighs)* I'll get the fly swatter.

FIRST ACTOR: You'll need something bigger than a fly swatter. Like a baseball bat. Or a bazooka. A bazooka would be good.

SECOND ACTOR: Aren't you a bit old to be so afraid of one tiny little... *(Sees it)* SweetJellyMattress! What is that thing?!

FIRST ACTOR: Told ya. Nuclear experiment gone wrong.

SECOND ACTOR: Or someone's been feeding it vitamin-enhanced steroids. I don't usually think of insects as tall, but that thing could play for the NBA. And it's got an Ick Factor of ten-point-infinity!

FIRST ACTOR: It's looking at you. With those dark googly eyes. It's looking right at you!

SECOND ACTOR: Don't show it any fear.

FIRST ACTOR: Too late. What do we do now?

SECOND ACTOR: Well, we can act like adults, and you can go right over there and step on it.

FIRST ACTOR: Me? Why not you? You've got the bigger feet. And the uglier shoes. Besides, stepping on a spider that big might only make it angry.

SECOND ACTOR:	Then that leaves us with two choices. We can either move to a different city…or run over it with the car.
FIRST ACTOR:	I'll get the keys. I hear Seattle's lovely this time of year.

112.

FIRST ACTOR:	*(Cuddling. Then sits up)* What was that?
SECOND ACTOR:	What was what?
FIRST ACTOR:	You purred.
SECOND ACTOR:	Excuse me?
FIRST ACTOR:	You purred. You were purring. Like a cat. *(Makes purring sound)*
SECOND ACTOR:	You're crazy.
FIRST ACTOR:	No use denying it. I heard you. You stretched, then snuggled right up to my shoulder and you purred. You know what that means?
SECOND ACTOR:	I'm getting in touch with my feline side?
FIRST ACTOR:	It means you are comfortable with me. Content. It means you really like me.
SECOND ACTOR:	You got all that from one little purr, huh?
FIRST ACTOR:	You like me. You like me so much, you purr. I know my pet sounds.
SECOND ACTOR:	Hmm. *(Flirtatiously)* Just wait until you hear me growl. *Gerrr-Rowrl.*
FIRST ACTOR:	Wow. That is not even in the same neighborhood as attractive.
SECOND ACTOR:	Sorry. Overreached. I'll stick to purring.
FIRST ACTOR:	Good idea.

113.

FIRST ACTOR: Is this seat taken?

SECOND ACTOR: Yes. By my boyfriend.

FIRST ACTOR: Your boyfriend?

SECOND ACTOR: I mean, my husband.

FIRST ACTOR: That's funny. You're not wearing a ring.

SECOND ACTOR: I don't like to be showy. It's a three-hundred-and-forty carat diamond. And you know how jealous all the masses can get.

FIRST ACTOR: Makes sense. So this husband of yours…

SECOND ACTOR: You mean Crusher?

FIRST ACTOR: Crusher?

SECOND ACTOR: He's six-five and leader of a psychotic ex-con biker gang. He just ducked into the restroom to strangle somebody.

FIRST ACTOR: I guess that explains what you see in him. Crusher aside, I couldn't help noticing that, here you are, a very sexy single woman sitting all by herself. Why is that?

SECOND ACTOR: Most men are intimidated by a woman who is vastly superior to them in every way. So completely out of their league.

FIRST ACTOR: Like you and me, for example.

SECOND ACTOR: Exactly… Either that, or it's my six highly contagious diseases, the loaded gun I carry, or the "I eat wimps for breakfast' tattoo on my left shoulder.

FIRST ACTOR: That dress hides it well.

SECOND ACTOR: This old thing? I stole it from my aunt's closet while she was dying of swine flu.

FIRST ACTOR: You're not going to make this easy on me, are you?

SECOND ACTOR: Not at all. *(Smiles seductively)* But I'm worth it…

114.

FIRST ACTOR: Those your parents?

SECOND ACTOR: Mostly.

FIRST ACTOR: What do you mean, mostly?

SECOND ACTOR: That's my old stepmom over there with her new boyfriend.

FIRST ACTOR: The blonde?

SECOND ACTOR: This week. My dad and Tricia are over there, kissing by the Coke machine.

FIRST ACTOR: Gross.

SECOND ACTOR: They're newlyweds. That's Mom number three for me.

FIRST ACTOR: You're lucky. I'm on Dad number four…Five, if you count Walter, who only moved in for six months, before Mom threw him out after she caught him texting his ex-wife. He tried to deny it, but she had a detective pull the phone records. After that, she started dating the detective.

SECOND ACTOR: I give Tricia no more than three years before she dumps my Dad. She used recycled wedding invitations with a 'fill in the blank' for the groom's name.

FIRST ACTOR: Not a good sign.

SECOND ACTOR: But I think my Dad's prepared for it. He still has his dating profile up on six different apps. Well, that I know of. Including one for people in sketchy marriages called *eTemporarily*.

FIRST ACTOR: Did you hear that Angie Peterson still has the original parents she was born with? And she's like, what… fifteen years old?

SECOND ACTOR: The same two parents? That's kinda creepy.

FIRST ACTOR: Yeah. It's pretty embarrassing. That girl's gonna need some serious therapy when she gets older…

115.

FIRST ACTOR: Hi, there!

SECOND ACTOR: What?

FIRST ACTOR: I said Hi there! How are you doing? It's great to see you!

SECOND ACTOR: Uh oh. Perky alert.

FIRST ACTOR: What? Who's perky? You and I are the only ones… oh, you mean me.

SECOND ACTOR: Perky and perceptive.

FIRST ACTOR: What's wrong with being perky, Mister Frowny Face?

SECOND ACTOR: Nothing…if you're a Disney cartoon downing Red Bull and Espresso shooters. For real live actual people, it's like a plague. An epidemic of enthusiasm.

FIRST ACTOR: There's nothing wrong with being a little…

SECOND ACTOR: Don't worry. I hear they're close to finding a cure for perkiness. Something to do with Swedish nihilism and recurring cellulite.

FIRST ACTOR: Is that supposed to be funny?

SECOND ACTOR: Supposed to be.

FIRST ACTOR: Oh, I get it. You're one of those Debbie Downer people, aren't you?

SECOND ACTOR: Hard to say. I'm usually too depressed to read my resume. Better to just sit here and sigh meaningfully for a month or two.

FIRST ACTOR: I know exactly what you need. Fresh baked cookies! My Grandmother's favorite recipe for cynicism.

SECOND ACTOR: Please, just kill me now.

FIRST ACTOR: Not gonna happen, cupcake. Now, where are all those tickle spots of yours? Huh? Where are those tickle spots?!

116.

FIRST ACTOR: Will you marry me?

SECOND ACTOR: Why would I want to do that?

FIRST ACTOR: Uh, that wasn't exactly the answer I was expecting.

SECOND ACTOR: Why would you even ask me something like that?

FIRST ACTOR: Why? Because I love you. Because I want to spend the rest of my life with you. Because you are the most amazing person I have ever met, and I can't live without you!

SECOND ACTOR: And that's it?

FIRST ACTOR: What more do you want me to say?

SECOND ACTOR: Say what you really want.

FIRST ACTOR: I just did.

SECOND ACTOR: I don't believe a word of it.

FIRST ACTOR: You don't believe I love you?

SECOND ACTOR: Of course, you love me. You'd be an idiot not to. And of course, you want to spend the rest of your life with me, because you are sick and tired of hanging out with those loser friends of yours.

FIRST ACTOR: My friends aren't losers!

SECOND ACTOR: Fred the Freak... Scott the Snotman...

FIRST ACTOR: I'll give you those. But some of my friends aren't losers.

SECOND ACTOR: Probably the ones I haven't met. Now tell me the real reason. Why do you want to marry me?

FIRST ACTOR: I...

SECOND ACTOR: *(interrupts him)* The *real* reason.

FIRST ACTOR: Your fully funded 401k.

SECOND ACTOR: I thought so.

117.

FIRST ACTOR: Anything on TV tonight?

SECOND ACTOR: No. *(They both sit and watch anyway)*

FIRST ACTOR: You left your underwear on the floor again.

SECOND ACTOR: Did I?

FIRST ACTOR: You do it to annoy me. Don't think I don't know that's why you do it.

SECOND ACTOR: Guess underwear and subtlety don't mix.

FIRST ACTOR: What happened to us, Earl?

SECOND ACTOR: I don't know. Dirty clothes. Gravity. Seems inevitable.

FIRST ACTOR: I don't mean the underwear… I mean what the hell happened to *us*?

SECOND ACTOR: I don't know. My beer belly. Your boobs. Gravity. Seems inevitable.

FIRST ACTOR: Tell me this… Is there anything about me you still love? Is there?

SECOND ACTOR: Give me a minute.

FIRST ACTOR: It shouldn't take a minute! You should be able to rattle off half a dozen lovable things about me in a heartbeat!

SECOND ACTOR: Well, if you had half a dozen lovable things, maybe I could. *(Sees her hurt expression)* I'm sorry. I was trying to be funny. Or stupid. Or male, which is all the same thing. *(Pause)* I…I love your meatloaf.

FIRST ACTOR: That's romantic. I think Shakespeare wrote a sonnet about that once.

SECOND ACTOR: Come on, Edna…

FIRST ACTOR: Or maybe it was it a poem by Emily Dickinson? *"Ode To Her Meatloaf"* It might even have been Percy Bysshe Shelly during his Casserole Period…

SECOND ACTOR: You're smarter than me. I ain't never even heard of Percy Bysshe Shelly before I met you. If he didn't write for *Car & Driver* magazine, I wouldn't of heard of him at all. And I guarantee you, nobody going by the name of 'Percy Bysshe' ever wrote for *Car & Driver*.

FIRST ACTOR: That's two. Smart and meatloaf. It's practically my Match.com profile.

SECOND ACTOR: Okay, you're funny, even when you're not trying to be. You have this cute way of squenching your eyes and throwing your hair back when you yawn that makes you look like a five-year-old. You put food out for robins in the winter, then yell at 'em all summer for pooping on the gas grill. You can't say no to any kid selling Girl Scout cookies or overpriced candy, even though we got three whole shelves stocked full of 'em. You can't sing worth a damn, but still do in the car, or when you think nobody's around. Even after all these years, you still look damn sexy when I sneak a peek at you in the shower. And every night before you fall asleep, you throw an arm around me and cuddle up close, as if you're holding onto some handsome movie star, instead of this old fat guy who's been stealing the covers and farting in your bed for the last three decades. Oh, and that crooked little smile of yours still melts me. That half a dozen yet? Counting the meatloaf?

FIRST ACTOR: *(Stunned)* Why, Earl Henry Dobson! All these years, and I never knew you were a closet romantic!

SECOND ACTOR: I ain't a closet anything. And don't you go thinkin' this means I'm gonna start picking my underwear up off the floor!

FIRST ACTOR: You're nothin' but a lazy, old slob. *(Pause, they watch TV)* You want meatloaf tonight?

SECOND ACTOR: Sure.

118.

FIRST ACTOR: Does it hurt? The first time, I mean?

SECOND ACTOR: A little. But only for a minute. Especially if he's gentle.

FIRST ACTOR: Were you scared?

SECOND ACTOR: Kinda. But I thought about it for a long time. I knew this was something I wanted to do. Why are you asking?

FIRST ACTOR: I'm thinking of doing it, too.

SECOND ACTOR: Shut up! Your parents would kill you!

FIRST ACTOR: I'm not going to tell them. Is that bad of me?

SECOND ACTOR: Girl, don't go putting me in the middle of that drama! I know your Mom. She'd freak, if she found out!

FIRST ACTOR: That's why I'm not going to tell her.

SECOND ACTOR: Who are you going to do it with?

FIRST ACTOR: Mister Leechman. Angela told me he's clean and really good at it.

SECOND ACTOR: Angela should know. He was her first too. So, when are you going to do it?

FIRST ACTOR: Tonight. At the mall.

SECOND ACTOR: At the mall?

FIRST ACTOR: Yeah. That new earring shop at the mall is open until six. Mister Leechman said they use a special gun, and it takes less than a minute to get my ears pierced. I already picked out a pair of really pretty silver hoops.

SECOND ACTOR: Girl, you are going to look so good with pierced ears! Just don't go all wild with ten or twelve piercings like Angela did. That would really make your parents lose it.

FIRST ACTOR: No way. I'm not that crazy.

119.

FIRST ACTOR: So, how did the blind date go? Did you finally meet the perfect man?

SECOND ACTOR: Pretty close.

FIRST ACTOR: You're kidding? You actually had a blind date who wasn't a total loser?

SECOND ACTOR: I know. I was stunned. He's a fireman, six-foot-two, broad shoulders, black hair and dreamy blue eyes. He knocks on my door holding a single yellow rose. Then asks *permission* to kiss my hand. We walk out to his brand new, hundred and forty-thousand-dollar Ferrari...and he lets *me* drive!

FIRST ACTOR: He let you drive his Ferrari?!

SECOND ACTOR: Even though I told him I had never driven a stick shift in my life. He didn't even complain when I burned out the clutch.

FIRST ACTOR: Unbelievable. Then what happened?

SECOND ACTOR: He asked me the name of my favorite restaurant, so I told him the most expensive place I could think of. *Chez Indulgence*...He just smiled and said; 'No problem,' then called for reservations. I told him they didn't take reservations, but he asked for the maître d' *by name*... and we ended up with the best table in the place!

FIRST ACTOR: That's incredible.

SECOND ACTOR: After the most delicious dinner I have ever eaten, followed by a dessert of expensive chocolates, with even more expensive champagne...my dream date took me shoe shopping for the rest of the night!

FIRST ACTOR: Okay...you had me until the shoe shopping. No guy is that perfect. He stood you up, didn't he?

SECOND ACTOR: Third time in a row. Men are pigs.

FIRST ACTOR: You said it, sister.

120.

FIRST ACTOR: Hi.

SECOND ACTOR: Excuse me?

FIRST ACTOR: I said, hi. Hello. You know, the standard greeting when people see each other, or meet for the first time.

SECOND ACTOR: Do I know you?

FIRST ACTOR: Not yet. But I bet you'd like to.

SECOND ACTOR: Not really. Not at all, actually.

FIRST ACTOR: Why not? I'm pretty lovable once you get to know me.

SECOND ACTOR: What a shame I'm going to miss out on that experience.

FIRST ACTOR: Maybe not. When you get to know me, you'll probably find all others pale by comparison. And then where will you be? Thinking of me every moment of every day. *(Sighs)* That may be too much to ask of anyone.

SECOND ACTOR: You don't have to worry. I've stopped thinking about you already. It was no problem at all.

FIRST ACTOR: You're just saying that.

SECOND ACTOR: Of course, I'm just saying that. That's how people communicate. And now, you are just saying good-bye, and how sorry you are that you ever bothered me. Then I can go back to my very pleasant, before-I-ever-met-you, pre-interruption, life.

FIRST ACTOR: But look at how much more exciting your life has been just since I showed up.

SECOND ACTOR: You call this exciting?

FIRST ACTOR: It is for me. My heart is racing, my wits are sharpened, and in case you hadn't noticed, I'm breathing a little heavy.

SECOND ACTOR: Sounds like the flu. I suggest you get a shot as quickly as possible. Besides, I already know far too many heavy breathers.

FIRST ACTOR:	I'm sure you do. Especially dressed like that. So now that we have had our share of witty banter and charming conversation, how about dinner and a movie?
SECOND ACTOR:	I'm sorry. Do you collect rejections? Is this some twisted hobby of yours?
FIRST ACTOR:	Come on… you know you're not going to say no. You are intrigued, possibly hungry, and definitely attracted to me, I can see it in your eyes.
SECOND ACTOR:	That's an astigmatism. I need to have that fixed…but I suppose food might not be too bad… unless your egotistic chatter continues to spoil my appetite.
FIRST ACTOR:	I'll try not to let it. Chinese?
SECOND ACTOR:	No, I'm Italian. *(Smiles)* You'll have to be much more perceptive if you have any chance of winning me over.

121.

FIRST ACTOR:	I can't do this…
SECOND ACTOR:	Sure, you can. All it takes is a certain gymnastic skill, and the ability not to giggle while naked.
FIRST ACTOR:	I mean I just want everything to be perfect.
SECOND ACTOR:	It usually is…when I'm involved.
FIRST ACTOR:	Do you have an answer for everything? *(No reply)* I said do you… Oh, I get it. Very funny.
SECOND ACTOR:	Thanks. My goal is to amuse you to the brink of ecstasy. Now, if you don't mind, I know of a better use for your lips then talking. Kissing my face, for example. Big, soft, warm, fluttery kisses you'll be embarrassed about in the morning. The lippier, the better.
FIRST ACTOR:	Isn't there anything you take seriously?
SECOND ACTOR:	*(Suddenly serious)* Just you…Just us… Just this…
FIRST ACTOR:	Mmmmm. Good answer. Bring those lips over here…

122.

FIRST ACTOR: Welcome to Bewilder Burger! What can I get you today?

SECOND ACTOR: Uh, I'm not sure. I don't see a menu board.

FIRST ACTOR: We are not like the average fast food restaurants. We don't believe in all that corporate marketing overkill here at Bewilder Burger.

SECOND ACTOR: Uh, okay. Do you have a smaller menu I can look at?

FIRST ACTOR: No, we don't.

SECOND ACTOR: You don't have menus.

FIRST ACTOR: That is correct.

SECOND ACTOR: No, menu board, no small menus. No menus at all?

FIRST ACTOR: You seem to be fixated on this whole 'menu' thing.

SECOND ACTOR: I mean, um, okay…just give me a Bewilder Burger.

FIRST ACTOR: Excellent choice. What kind of faux digestible or inorganic consumable substitution would you prefer?

SECOND ACTOR: Uh, I don't know. Beef, I guess.

FIRST ACTOR: I'm sorry. We do not believe in using beef, or beef byproducts.

SECOND ACTOR: But you're a burger joint?

FIRST ACTOR: A 100% beef-free burger joint.

SECOND ACTOR: Okay. Do you have chicken?

FIRST ACTOR: Sorry.

SECOND ACTOR: Pork? Lamb? Goat? Venison? Bison?

FIRST ACTOR: We at Bewilder Burger do not believe in the slaughter of innocent wildlife just to feed your cruel, self-serving gluttonous hunger pains. But feel free to snatch up any defenseless animal you see wandering the neighborhood and tear it to pieces with your teeth. I hear most domesticated pets are notoriously easy to catch.

SECOND ACTOR: You realize you are being both insulting and condescending to the only customer in this place?

FIRST ACTOR: We at Bewilder Burger do not discriminate based on presence. We believe in being insulting and condescending to ferocious foodians, wherever they may be.

SECOND ACTOR: All right, wise guy. Just give me a veggie burger. And hold the sarcasm, if you don't mind.

FIRST ACTOR: We at Bewilder Burger refuse to be part of your savage desire to take the life of guiltless plants simply to satisfy your contemptuous herba-barbarious needs. Perhaps there is another life form you wish to oppress, murder or masticate?

SECOND ACTOR: Let me get this straight…You don't serve meat or vegetables? What kind of fast food restaurant is this?

FIRST ACTOR: We are not a fast food restaurant. We are a *fasting* food restaurant. You come here *not* to eat.

SECOND ACTOR: Not to eat?

FIRST ACTOR: Correct. You come here to fast.

SECOND ACTOR: A fasting food restaurant?

FIRST ACTOR: One of the finest.

SECOND ACTOR: You don't serve any food at all?

FIRST ACTOR: It would be against our Mission Statement and Corporate Philosophy.

SECOND ACTOR: How do you stay in business?

FIRST ACTOR: Tax credits. The Bewilder Burger concept started in California.

SECOND ACTOR: Well, that explains everything…

123.

FIRST ACTOR: Tell me a story.

SECOND ACTOR: What kind of story?

FIRST ACTOR: Oh, you know. A bedtime-type story. The kind you make up just for me.

SECOND ACTOR: Okay…Once upon a time…

FIRST ACTOR: You told that one before.

SECOND ACTOR: Not really. Most stories start with 'Once upon a time.'

FIRST ACTOR: Why?

SECOND ACTOR: Well, uh, because that's how you know it's make-believe and didn't just happen last week. Now, where was I? Once upon a time. In a galaxy far, far away…there lived a beautiful princess…

FIRST ACTOR: What color was her hair? Was she tall or short? What was her name? What did she look like?

SECOND ACTOR: Brown. Petite. Princess Magdalena. And she looked a lot like you.

FIRST ACTOR: I like her.

SECOND ACTOR: Good. Then maybe I can finish my story…

FIRST ACTOR: You haven't really started. Where does Princess Magdalena live?

SECOND ACTOR: In a castle. In a kingdom.

FIRST ACTOR: Not very specific. Stories should have details. Otherwise they're just make-believe.

SECOND ACTOR: She…uh, lived in an ancient stone castle. In the faraway land of Primordia.

FIRST ACTOR: Where's that?

SECOND ACTOR: Look it up on Google maps. So one day, Princess Magdalena was peeking out her castle window…

FIRST ACTOR:	Ancient stone castles don't have windows.
SECOND ACTOR:	This one did. She was looking out the large, double-paned, stained glass window when she saw…
FIRST ACTOR:	A giant? A lion? The man of her dreams?
SECOND ACTOR:	All of the above.
FIRST ACTOR:	That's not how you tell a story! You have to build up to it! Not throw everything in at once!
SECOND ACTOR:	You're not going to make this easy on me, are you? So beautiful little brunette Princess Magdalena of Primordia was looking out the large stained-glass window of her castle…
FIRST ACTOR:	Double-paned.
SECOND ACTOR:	The large, double-paned, stained-glass window…when she saw a giant, a lion and the man of her dreams walking across the field toward the ancient castle…
FIRST ACTOR:	This isn't one of your better stories.
SECOND ACTOR:	*(Frustrated)* Just wait until you hear what happens next… Princess Magdalena looked out the large *double-paned*, stained-glass windows, when she saw a giant, a lion and the man of her dreams walking across the field toward her ancient stone castle…
FIRST ACTOR:	You're being redundant.
SECOND ACTOR:	When suddenly, the lion growled, leapt straight in the air and ate the man of her dreams in one bite. The giant got so mad, he sat on the lion, crushing him instantly, but was so lonely, he jumped into the castle moat and drowned. The end.
FIRST ACTOR:	That's an awful story!
SECOND ACTOR:	Really? I kind of liked it. Sweet dreams!
FIRST ACTOR:	I'm telling Mommy!

124.

FIRST ACTOR: You're beautiful.

SECOND ACTOR: No, I'm not.

FIRST ACTOR: Yes, you are. You're absolutely perfect.

SECOND ACTOR: How can you say that?

FIRST ACTOR: How can you not see it?

SECOND ACTOR: I don't know. I guess because every other time anyone told me how wonderful I am, it doesn't take them long to tell me the opposite.

FIRST ACTOR: Then they are crazy.

SECOND ACTOR: Or consistent. I'm perfect, until they get to know me. Really know me. Then I'm nothing but a big bundle of flaws, faults, and everything that annoys them.

FIRST ACTOR: Sounds like their problem, not yours.

SECOND ACTOR: Maybe, but once I fall in love, it becomes my problem.

FIRST ACTOR: A problem worth having.

SECOND ACTOR: Easy for you to say. I don't think I can go through that again. Watching the respect and admiration in someone else's eyes slowly wither away and die.

FIRST ACTOR: Sorry. You can't dissuade or persuade me. I know not every love is real. Not every crush will last. And sometimes promises can bring more pain than happiness…

SECOND ACTOR: You know that you're not exactly helping here?

FIRST ACTOR: I'm trying to. What I mean is that, just because you've hit a few speed bumps, it doesn't mean you should push love out of your life. Saying you're never going to have these feelings again.

SECOND ACTOR: That's exactly what I'm saying.

FIRST ACTOR: And what I'm saying is…

SECOND ACTOR: Oh, no. Here it comes…

FIRST ACTOR: …I love you. No matter what happens. No matter how much pain it may cost me. I love you…and I need to know whether there is even the slightest chance you love me too.

SECOND ACTOR: Why are you doing this?

FIRST ACTOR: Because every part of my life is better with you in it. And every day I spend without you is killing me a little more.

SECOND ACTOR: So, we're talking pity love here?

FIRST ACTOR: You can choose to go wall yourself off from everyone and everything… or you can dump your cynicism and self-pity and make my life whole again. Your choice.

SECOND ACTOR: Hmmm. That's a tough one…

FIRST ACTOR: *(Hurt)* Really?

SECOND ACTOR: Hey, I'm kidding! I'll take door number two. The cuddly couple prize.

FIRST ACTOR: Good choice.

SECOND ACTOR: But keep this in mind… If you even think about falling *out* of love with me…I will hurt you. Seriously hurt you. I'm talking intestinal damage, and irreversible groin trauma. You got that?

FIRST ACTOR: Absolutely. Clear as a bell.

SECOND ACTOR: I mean it!

FIRST ACTOR: Irreversible groin trauma. Got it…

SECOND ACTOR: You better.

FIRST ACTOR: *(Smiles)* You're so cute when you're trying to be vicious…

125.

FIRST ACTOR: Life is crap.

SECOND ACTOR: No. Crap is crap. Life is just the way crap gets dumped on you.

FIRST ACTOR: You wouldn't believe the day I've had…

SECOND ACTOR: It can't be as bad as mine.

FIRST ACTOR: It was worse. Everything went wrong…

SECOND ACTOR: Wrong is nothing. I'm talking complete rejection. Shattered dreams. Utter disillusionment.

FIRST ACTOR: Why do you do that?

SECOND ACTOR: Do what?

FIRST ACTOR: Always have to try to make your day sound worse than mine. Like you have this desperate need to 'outwhine' me.

SECOND ACTOR: That's what friends are for.

FIRST ACTOR: Friendship is crap.

SECOND ACTOR: Tell me about it…

126.

FIRST ACTOR: We've got to do something about Mom.

SECOND ACTOR: It's not my problem.

FIRST ACTOR: Of course, it's your problem. She's your mother.

SECOND ACTOR: Not when she acts like that. Then she's your mom. I don't even know her.

FIRST ACTOR: This is my graduation party and she's dancing with all my friends.

SECOND ACTOR: Hitting on them too. She just whispered something to Josh Flannagan that made him spit his Dr. Pepper halfway across the room.

FIRST ACTOR: Aren't you embarrassed by her?

SECOND ACTOR: Every single day of my life. I think that's why she does it.

FIRST ACTOR: Wait a minute…is she dancing on the table? *(Calling out)* Mom! That table isn't strong enough it'll… MOM!

SECOND ACTOR: *(Sighs)* You get the ice. I'll call the hospital…. Again…

127.

FIRST ACTOR: Why are you smiling?

SECOND ACTOR: No reason.

FIRST ACTOR: No, c'mon. Tell me.

SECOND ACTOR: Tell you what?

FIRST ACTOR: What's going on? You have this big, twisted smile on your face like you just stole a million dollars, or set fire to your neighbor's cat.

SECOND ACTOR: Well, I'm not rich. And I don't have any lighter fluid.

FIRST ACTOR: So, what's up? Why the sneaky grin? What did you do?

SECOND ACTOR: Nothing. Absolutely nothing.

FIRST ACTOR: You're not going to tell me.?

SECOND ACTOR: There's nothing to tell.

FIRST ACTOR: And that's your story?

SECOND ACTOR: That's my story.

FIRST ACTOR: *(Walking off)* You can't fool me. I know you're up to something. I know there's a reason for that stupid smile. I just know it…

SECOND ACTOR: *(Smiling)* I just love to drive him crazy…

128.

FIRST ACTOR: Stop it!

SECOND ACTOR: Stop what?

FIRST ACTOR: You know.

SECOND ACTOR: No, I don't know. If I knew what I was doing wrong, I'd stop it in a heartbeat.

FIRST ACTOR: See? You're doing it again.

SECOND ACTOR: Doing what? What am I doing?

FIRST ACTOR: Being nice. You do it just to annoy me!

SECOND ACTOR: I'm being nice just to annoy you?

FIRST ACTOR: Don't even think of denying it.

SECOND ACTOR: I… I'm… You're kidding, right?

FIRST ACTOR: Now you're being condescending. That's very not nice, you overly considerate creep!

SECOND ACTOR: Let me get this straight…You're mad at me because I'm being too nice, but when I find that hard to believe, then I'm *not* being nice, and you get even madder at me?

FIRST ACTOR: See? That is so…you! I share my innermost feelings about what a viciously thoughtful person you can be, then you go and make it sound ridiculous! Thanks a lot, Mr. Pseudo-Perfect-Butthead!

SECOND ACTOR: Please…Just tell me what it is you want from me? You want me to be nice? Not nice? Not listen to what you say? Or simply stand here and be rude and oblivious? I need to know what exactly you want me to do?

FIRST ACTOR: I want you to love me! That's all.

SECOND ACTOR: I do. I do love you! I've always loved you!

FIRST ACTOR: Why?

SECOND ACTOR: Why?

FIRST ACTOR: Yes, why? Give me reasons. Really good ones.

SECOND ACTOR: Reasons why I love you?

FIRST ACTOR: The first fifteen that pop into your head. That shouldn't be too hard.

SECOND ACTOR: Okay, well, um…I love you because… you, uh…

FIRST ACTOR: Come on. Spit 'em out!

SECOND ACTOR: Because… you, um…make my life interesting.

FIRST ACTOR: Really? That's all you got? I ask for fifteen little reasons, and all you can come up with is that you love me because I make your life interesting? What? Like I'm your personal equivalent of Wikipedia or the National Geographic Channel, or something?

SECOND ACTOR: No! Yes! I don't know… The truth is I'm pretty much terrified to say anything else to you.

FIRST ACTOR: Nice. Real nice.

SECOND ACTOR: Wait…Is that a good nice, or the bad nice?

FIRST ACTOR: *(Walking away)* Even nicer.

SECOND ACTOR: That's good, isn't it? Or is it? Uh, did I mention that I love you?

FIRST ACTOR: I hope your lips get so chapped, they fall off! That might make your life more *interesting*.

SECOND ACTOR: You don't really mean that, do you? *(Follows offstage)* Honey? Sweetheart? Crazy person?

129.

FIRST ACTOR: There you are. I've been looking for you.

SECOND ACTOR: I was hoping you'd find me.

FIRST ACTOR: There's a train I'd like you to catch. Face first, if I can help it.

SECOND ACTOR: Always the stupid little threats. What's the matter? The 'original' setting on your brain still broken? You lose the instruction manual or somethin'?

FIRST ACTOR: Man, you are so close to a horrible death, I can almost smell it.

SECOND ACTOR: The only thing horrible thing I smell around here is you. But hey, consistency was always your best feature. And speaking of consistency, why don't you go do something completely out of character and make people happy. Preferably by choking on your own bile.

FIRST ACTOR: Sorry. Got a lot of things to do first. And most of them involve strangling you with your own intestines. So what do you say we get started?

SECOND ACTOR: Anytime you're ready, tough guy. Just give me a reason.

FIRST ACTOR: I know how your little mind works. Reason's got nothing to do with it.

SECOND ACTOR: Leave the smart comments to someone who thinks. I'll have you know I make my living grinding vermin like you into the dust.

FIRST ACTOR: You couldn't make a living if you were the only sheep at a bestiality convention.

SECOND ACTOR: I should have expected something that disgusting from you. Of course, you were probably the guest speaker at that convention.

FIRST ACTOR: One of these days, I'm going to kill you.

SECOND ACTOR: I'd like to see you try.

FIRST ACTOR: The only thing I hate more than you…is these family reunions.

SECOND ACTOR: Yeah. Did you say hi to Mom yet?

FIRST ACTOR: Naw. I don't think I can take that much hostility.

130.

FIRST ACTOR: Two minutes to curtain. Are you nervous?

SECOND ACTOR: Not at all.

FIRST ACTOR: Are you lying?

SECOND ACTOR: Absolutely. But to tell the truth, I've been waiting for this my whole life. I worked hard to get here, and I really do deserve this award.

FIRST ACTOR: I was thinking the same thing… Only about myself.

SECOND ACTOR: I agree. You deserve to be nominated. Other than my work, you were way ahead of everyone else.

FIRST ACTOR: Other than your work?

SECOND ACTOR: Honesty is a fault of mine.

FIRST ACTOR: One of many, I'm sure. But that's okay. It'll just make your shock that much stronger when they announce my name as the winner.

SECOND ACTOR: That would be a shock. But nothing that a few months of intensive self-delusion therapy won't help you get over.

FIRST ACTOR: Too bad this isn't a sarcasm and narcissism contest. You'd be sure to win. By the way, what was your name again? Oh, doesn't matter. I've forgotten you already.

131.

FIRST ACTOR: Are you going to eat that?

SECOND ACTOR: I plan to. That is pretty much why I ordered it.

FIRST ACTOR: I don't think you'll like it.

SECOND ACTOR: What's not to like? It smells fantastic. The meat is cooked to perfection. The vegetables are just the right consistency. Steamed to a soft, yet surprisingly crunchy goodness. The spices are subtle, yet savory. And this honey garlic wine sauce is pure heaven. So yeah, it's everything I can do not to drop my mouth to the plate and trough out like a hungry heifer.

FIRST ACTOR: That dish is overflowing with calories.

SECOND ACTOR: I know. Amazingly tasty calories. I'm guessing about two thousand of them. Each one even more delicious then the last.

FIRST ACTOR: Aren't you worried you'll get fat?

SECOND ACTOR: Possibly, but I'll risk it. It's the least I can do for my taste buds. They've been with me my whole life, and I kind of feel I owe them.

FIRST ACTOR: But think of your cholesterol!

SECOND ACTOR: Hard to do, when my senses are so joyously overcome with absolute culinary delight. All I can think of is how glad I am that I'm not on a diet, and forced to order a plain, sad salad. Like yours, for instance.

FIRST ACTOR: I hope you choke on that forkful.

SECOND ACTOR: You know the best cure for jealousy? This honey garlic wine sauce. Soooo much better than a plain, sad salad. Yum. Yummy. Sigh. Oh, you better eat your plain, sad salad before it gets…I don't know…wilted.

FIRST ACTOR: You are a cruel human being.

SECOND ACTOR: I'll try to digest that fact. This honey garlic wine sauce should help…

132.

FIRST ACTOR: How are you today?

SECOND ACTOR: Not interested. Not responding.

FIRST ACTOR: That's perfectly understandable. You don't know me, but I just had to come up and say hello to you. I couldn't help myself. You know what I mean?

SECOND ACTOR: No. And I'm pretty sure I don't want to.

FIRST ACTOR: I was thinking that this may be one of those moments, one of those rare opportunities in life, when you see someone and *BAM*, you know from the very first look that this is a person who can totally change your life.

SECOND ACTOR: I'm sorry. I'm not in the life-changing business at the moment. In fact, I'm having enough trouble trying to handle the complete devastation I've made of my own life to even think about getting caught up in yours.

FIRST ACTOR: You already are. My life changed the instant I saw you.

SECOND ACTOR: Then change it back.

FIRST ACTOR: Too late. I'm smitten, can't you tell?

SECOND ACTOR: Can't tell. Don't care. Need to be alone.

FIRST ACTOR: You don't mean that. I could feel your vibes all the way across the room. And it touched me. Like I've been touched by an angel. Shaken to the core. My world has been thoroughly rocked, and you can't unchange an experience like that. It would be like trying to put the genie back into the bottle.

SECOND ACTOR: Then let me make this easy for you. I'm no genie and I'm nobody's angel. I'm sorry if your core got shaken and your world rocked, but you need to get yourself unsmitten and step away from my personal space. Or I'll happily change you into a permanent soprano. And that's one life-changing experience you don't want. *(Cuts off his reply)* You have my permission to disappear now.

133.

FIRST ACTOR: Looking for something?

SECOND ACTOR: Oh, man…You scared me to death!

FIRST ACTOR: That would be an unpleasant way to die.

SECOND ACTOR: Wait a minute. You look familiar. Do I know you?

FIRST ACTOR: You should.

SECOND ACTOR: No… It couldn't be…

FIRST ACTOR: But it is.

SECOND ACTOR: What do you want from me?!

FIRST ACTOR: I think you know.

SECOND ACTOR: Get back! Don't come any closer! I'm warning you!

FIRST ACTOR: You are warning me? I would say that is rather amusing, don't you think?

SECOND ACTOR: Please…just leave me alone.

FIRST ACTOR: It's a little late for that.

SECOND ACTOR: It wasn't me. I swear I had nothing to do with it! Nothing at all!

FIRST ACTOR: I am terribly sorry, but I don't believe you. And even if I did…I really don't care. It happened, and now somebody has to pay.

SECOND ACTOR: Pay? But I…I don't have any money.

FIRST ACTOR: That would be unfortunate.

SECOND ACTOR: Are you…are you going to kill me?

FIRST ACTOR: The IRS doesn't work like that. But I can promise you that settling these back taxes is going to be the most excruciatingly painful thing you have ever experienced.

SECOND ACTOR: Noooooooooo!

134.

FIRST ACTOR: It's official! Everything in this house hates me!

SECOND ACTOR: I don't.

FIRST ACTOR: Everything mechanical. I use the can opener, and the only thing it opens is a vein in my finger… I pull out the vacuum cleaner, and it spews out ten times more dirt than it picks up… I just walk into a room and another light bulb burns out!

SECOND ACTOR: Light bulbs aren't mechanical.

FIRST ACTOR: Then everything mechanical *and* electrical hates me!

SECOND ACTOR: Don't forget your effect on plumbing. The faucet you broke. And the toilet that keeps overflowing…

FIRST ACTOR: Are you *trying* to make me feel better?

SECOND ACTOR: Don't think so. I'm pretty much siding with the appliances here.

FIRST ACTOR: I can break you too, you know.

SECOND ACTOR: I have no doubt.

135.

FIRST ACTOR: There are so many things I miss about our relationship.

SECOND ACTOR: That's funny. I can't think of a single thing.

FIRST ACTOR: Sure, you do. The jokes. The excitement. The late-night cuddling…

SECOND ACTOR: The screaming. The jealousy. The cruelty. The paranoia.

FIRST ACTOR: Oh, come on. It wasn't that bad.

SECOND ACTOR: Maybe. But it wasn't that good either.

FIRST ACTOR: I guess I remember it differently. I choose to focus on the positive.

SECOND ACTOR: Yeah. And somewhere Adolph Hitler is looking back at World War II and thinking, "Good times…"

136.

FIRST ACTOR: Hey, whatta you say, you and I go out and do something really bizarre tonight! Something so wild, unpredictable, and completely crazy, that people will be talking about it for months. Years maybe!

SECOND ACTOR: I'm sorry. Do I know you?

FIRST ACTOR: No. That's what'll be so crazy about it! You and me, total strangers out looking for danger! Oh, man…it'll be epic! Digitally epic!

SECOND ACTOR: Look, I don't know who you are…

FIRST ACTOR: Ronnie.

SECOND ACTOR: Okay, Ronnie…I still don't know anything about you, and besides, I'm married.

FIRST ACTOR: Not tonight you're not. That's what'll be so insane! Digitally insane! You and me. No spouses. No criticism and no boundaries. Nothing to hold us back! Look out, world! Ronnie and what's-er-name are on the prowl! Grrrrrroooooooowwwwllll!

SECOND ACTOR: You have a serious disconnection with reality. Do you know that?

FIRST ACTOR: *(Pause, then)* Actually, it's just the opposite. The sad truth is…I'm a bookkeeper, and not a very good one. In fact, I am pretty much the joke of the office. I'm stuck in a lifeless marriage with two rude teenagers, who ignore everything I say. My life is dry, meaningless and completely lacking in spontaneity. I have to do one fun thing…just one out-of-character thing before I die, or I swear to God, my head will explode, my soul will shrivel up, and all those things they say about me behind my back will be true…

SECOND ACTOR: Okay. Wow, I didn't mean to…

FIRST ACTOR:	It's okay...Nobody takes me seriously. Or listens to me at all. I was hoping that...just maybe... a total stranger might...I dunno... It was a stupid idea. Sorry I bothered you. *(Turns to leave)*
SECOND ACTOR:	*(Pause)* Hey, Ronnie... Did you ever sneak into a field and tip a cow in the moonlight?
FIRST ACTOR:	Now you're talking! It'll be epic! Digitally epic!

137.

FIRST ACTOR:	I got the part!
SECOND ACTOR:	You got the part? That's great! Congratulations! When do you start?
FIRST ACTOR:	I don't know yet.
SECOND ACTOR:	Well, what did they say?
FIRST ACTOR:	Nothing yet. But I just know I got the part. I was so much better than all those others who tried out. Some were really pitiful. And ugly? It looked like a kennel.
SECOND ACTOR:	So they were going for looks? That's all?
FIRST ACTOR:	No. They had me read a whole bunch of lines and things. But the director couldn't stop smiling through my whole read. Like he was so happy, he even burst out laughing in the middle of it.
SECOND ACTOR:	But I thought it was a serious role? Weren't you supposed to be dying of some terrible disease?
FIRST ACTOR:	Yeah. And I think it surprised him when I hit the floor and flailed around for ten whole minutes before I died. The cameraman even had to cover his mouth and leave the room, he was so moved.
SECOND ACTOR:	I bet.
FIRST ACTOR:	Maybe I should start practicing my award speech...

138.

FIRST ACTOR: Pssssst. What's the answer to question three?

SECOND ACTOR: Shut up.

FIRST ACTOR: The answer to three is 'shut up?' I don't think so.

SECOND ACTOR: Ssssshh.

FIRST ACTOR: Ssssshh is the capital of Uruguay? That doesn't even sound Spanish. What about number twelve? The first line of the Gettysburg Address?

SECOND ACTOR: The teacher is watching.

FIRST ACTOR: Really? Lincoln was worried about what his teacher saw?

SECOND ACTOR: This is a test. We're not supposed to be talking.

FIRST ACTOR: Then how am I supposed to find out the answers?

SECOND ACTOR: Study. Read the book. Come to class once in a while.

FIRST ACTOR: Why? You did all that and you think 'Ssssshh' is the capital of Uruguay and Abraham Lincoln was worried about his teacher in the middle of the Civil War.

SECOND ACTOR: If I give you the answers, will you shut up before you get us both in trouble?

FIRST ACTOR: Cross my heart and hope to pass.

SECOND ACTOR: Okay... Then the Capital of Uruguay is Narnia, and the first line of the Gettysburg Address is "Friends, Romans, Countrymen. Lend me your ears."

FIRST ACTOR: Thanks.

SECOND ACTOR: No problem.

139.

FIRST ACTOR: How are you…? Uh-oh. I know that look.

SECOND ACTOR: What look?

FIRST ACTOR: The 'gob-smacked, inner tsunami, swept away by your latest instantaneous obsession' look.

SECOND ACTOR: I don't do that!

FIRST ACTOR: We'll see. So, who or what is it this time?

SECOND ACTOR: Well, since you asked… she is a who, not a what. And you've got to meet her!

FIRST ACTOR: Who?

SECOND ACTOR: My muse! My inspiration. The one person who broke through all that garbage that was cluttering up my head and got me inspired again.

FIRST ACTOR: One woman did all that?

SECOND ACTOR: That's right. I started talking to her, and *BOOM!* All these ideas and everything just started flowing out. Like she freed some clogged-up valve in my soul.

FIRST ACTOR And how long did you know this woman before she unclogged you?

SECOND ACTOR: It's not about time. It's about inspiration!

FIRST ACTOR You knew her exactly how long?

SECOND ACTOR: Okay, okay. Nine and a half minutes. Just two bus stops, but she did it. She freed me. She's my muse!

FIRST ACTOR That is the last time I let you ride the bus alone.

140.

FIRST ACTOR: I'm fat.

SECOND ACTOR: No, you're not.

FIRST ACTOR: Look at me! I'm two pounds south of grotesque.

SECOND ACTOR: Here we go again…

FIRST ACTOR: And I'm old. I'm as wrinkled as a prune left in the washing machine for a week.

SECOND ACTOR: You look fine to me.

FIRST ACTOR: I don't want to look 'fine!' Wines are fine, and they are purple and aged. When you say people look fine, it means they still have a couple of teeth, a little hair, and their breasts are barely dragging on the floor.

SECOND ACTOR: At least you wouldn't have to sweep the floor as often. That's a plus.

FIRST ACTOR: I hate you. I hate me. I hate my face. Did I mention that I hate you?

SECOND ACTOR: Consistently. But I love you anyway.

FIRST ACTOR: What could you possibly love about me? I'm a fat, soggy prune with long, saggy boobs.

SECOND ACTOR: That's not what I see.

FIRST ACTOR: Oh, and what do you see, Mister Glaucoma?

SECOND ACTOR: I see a woman in the shape of an angel. Someone so far out of my league, who scowls at herself, but always finds a reason to smile at me. Most of the time, anyway. Whose soft, beautiful eyes only sees faults in herself, never in others. I see a dream I had since I was young, miraculously entering my life. And even more miraculously, choosing to stay with me, when anyone with any sense or taste would probably have dumped my sorry butt long ago.

FIRST ACTOR: I meant to. I got busy. And there were all those Gilligan's Island reruns to binge watch...

SECOND ACTOR: I see this warm and weird and wonderful bundle of anxieties making my laugh and smile...and making me feel I'm about as blessed as a man can be. That's what I see every time I look at you.

FIRST ACTOR: Really?

SECOND ACTOR: Really.

FIRST ACTOR: I kind of like the way you lie.

SECOND ACTOR: I kind of like the way you look. Can't help it. You're much too cute to shoot.

FIRST ACTOR: You know, that somehow managed to be both sweet and creepy at the same time.

SECOND ACTOR: Poetry was never my thing. Sorry if I ruined the moment.

FIRST ACTOR: That's okay. I'll have it written into the Emergency Protection Order.

SECOND ACTOR: It would take more than that to keep me away from you, gorgeous.

FIRST ACTOR: Once again. Sweet and creepy. This would be a good time to shut up and kiss me.

SECOND ACTOR: I can't.

FIRST ACTOR: Why not?

SECOND ACTOR: Well, you are kind of fat... *(Yelps with pain)* Ow! I'm kidding! It was a joke. Owww! Stop hitting me! OWWWWWW!

141.

FIRST ACTOR: Let's talk about when you're planning to marry me.

SECOND ACTOR: Say what?

FIRST ACTOR: Marry me. Commit your life to me. Promise eternal wedding bliss. Foreswear all others and only see me naked for the entire rest of your life.

SECOND ACTOR: Are you crazy?

FIRST ACTOR: Maybe, but we're talking 'for better or worse' here, so crazy is technically irrelevant. But sometimes crazy can be good...like I'm crazy about you. Although I have to admit, crazy can be bad, too. Very bad... Very, very bad... Crazy bad. *(Brightens)* So what do you say? Wedding on Saturday? Ten AM work for you?

SECOND ACTOR: What are you talking about?! I barely know you.

FIRST ACTOR: That is such an overused excuse. I mean, does anybody really 'know' another person? Except for in the conjugal or Biblical sense, and we can take care of that after we are married. Almost immediately after, since you are so darn cute. Can't wait to see you in a tux. *(Giggles)* Or out of one. Do you have the wedding party picked out yet?

SECOND ACTOR: What wedding party?

FIRST ACTOR: You know, Best Man. Ushers. Half a dozen friends and family members you can barely stand, and probably haven't talked to in years, but you have to put them in your wedding party, because they had you in theirs, or you promised them when you were twelve, and Great Aunt Bertha will never forgive you if you don't... Now tell me. Are we talking a big churchy affair here, or a small intimate ceremony? I'm good either way.

SECOND ACTOR: Okay. You obviously have me confused with someone else...

FIRST ACTOR: No, I don't. You are my fiancée.

SECOND ACTOR: No, I'm not! I am not anyone's fiancée. We are ten minutes into a blind date, that I got roped into as a favor to my urologist's first cousin. And suddenly, you are proposing to me?

FIRST ACTOR: And?

SECOND ACTOR: And, what?

FIRST ACTOR: And what does any of that have to do with our upcoming nuptials?

SECOND ACTOR: Listen, lady. You have issues. Serious issues.

FIRST ACTOR: Not really. Just a fiancée with cold feet. But I hear it happens all the time. You'll be fine after the honeymoon.

SECOND ACTOR: You are definitely weirding me out. I have to get out of here. And clearly, you are way late for your medication.

FIRST ACTOR: Did I mention I was rich? Or at least my family is, so I guess that sort of makes me rich, too.

SECOND ACTOR: *(Hesitates, then)* Really? Um… How rich?

FIRST ACTOR: I don't know. Jeff Bezos rich. Bill Gates and Warren Buffet rich. Saudi Arabian prince rich. Or at least that's what our private banker tells us. He flew in last week on the family jet. Something about a big jump in my trust fund. *(Shrugs)* I'm not all that good with numbers over ten figures.

SECOND ACTOR: Uh huh. *(Pause)* Actually, Saturday morning at ten works for me.

FIRST ACTOR: Great. I have the tux shop on speed-dial. I'm thinking burgundy crushed velvet cummerbunds.

SECOND ACTOR: Whatever you say, darling. Uh, any chance I can meet this private banker? Or see your credit score, maybe?

142.

FIRST ACTOR: I hate housework. *(No answer)* Hey, I'm talking to you!

SECOND ACTOR: I heard you. You hate housework.

FIRST ACTOR: That's right. Hate all of it. The vacuuming. The dusting. The dishes. The laundry.

SECOND ACTOR: And that's why you refuse to do any of it.

FIRST ACTOR: Darn right. It's demeaning.

SECOND ACTOR: Of course, it's demeaning. That's why you make me do it all. The vacuuming. The dusting. Dishes. The laundry.

FIRST ACTOR: Are you complaining?

SECOND ACTOR: Why would I complain, when I get to vacuum, dusting, do the dishes, and laundry? My life is just about perfect.

FIRST ACTOR: That sounds an awful lot like sarcasm to me.

SECOND ACTOR: Sorry. No time for sarcasm. The rug needs vacuuming. Gosh, I feel fulfilled. Too bad I wasted all those years in college and grad school getting my PhD. Especially when I could have gotten my Doctorate in Dusting.

145.

FIRST ACTOR: I am going to tear you apart.

SECOND ACTOR: You're going to try.

FIRST ACTOR: No matter what you do, you are done. Finished. Over. Dead man walking. It's 'kiss-the-baby good-night, Lights-out and fade-to-black' time.

SECOND ACTOR: *(Facetiously)* Ooooooh. I'm scared.

FIRST ACTOR: When I'm done with you, you'll have more scars than a recycled piñata. It'll look like the garbage disposal backed up month-old leftover sushi.

SECOND ACTOR: It takes more than talk. Make your move, tough guy.

FIRST ACTOR: You asked for it… Pawn to king four.

SECOND ACTOR: Ooooooh. I'm scared.

144.

FIRST ACTOR: Look at me. I said look at me!

SECOND ACTOR: What? I am looking at you.

FIRST ACTOR: I know when you're not telling the truth.

SECOND ACTOR: What makes you think I'm not telling you the truth?

FIRST ACTOR: Easy. You have all these little quirks you do when you're lying. First, you look down at my shoulders, instead of my eyes.

SECOND ACTOR: So? You have nice shoulders. I've always admired how they, uh…attach to your arms so well.

FIRST ACTOR: Second, you make really lame excuses. Third, you shuffle back in forth on your feet, like you have to pee.

SECOND ACTOR: Maybe I have to pee.

FIRST ACTOR: Or maybe you're lying. See? Shoulder. Excuse. Shuffle. You're busted. Now tell me the truth.

SECOND ACTOR: Okay. Your kids aren't precious. They are monsters. Criminals in training. Satisfied? Good eye contact. No excuse. No pee pee dance. Now you probably hate me.

FIRST ACTOR: I'm not going to lie about it…

145.

FIRST ACTOR: Drinking alone?

SECOND ACTOR: In a perfect universe.

FIRST ACTOR: I'm Walter. Is this seat taken?

SECOND ACTOR: No. But I am. Feel free to take that chair with you when you leave.

FIRST ACTOR: How about if I buy you a drink?

SECOND ACTOR: Only if you'll do it from across the room.

FIRST ACTOR: Cute. Y'know, you look familiar. Have we met before?

SECOND ACTOR: No. But you do remind me of a fungus I once grew in biology lab.

FIRST ACTOR: You're funny.

SECOND ACTOR: Yeah. My Mom was bitten by a clown when she was pregnant. I must have inherited the gene.

FIRST ACTOR: Must have been a really good-looking clown. You're the most beautiful woman in this place.

SECOND ACTOR: You should have seen me before I got the big red nose fixed. Haven't been able to do anything about the size eighty-eight floppy feet though.

FIRST ACTOR: I love a woman with a sense of humor. But don't feel you have to play so hard to get.

SECOND ACTOR: I'm not playing hard to get. I'm playing impossible to get. And for some reason, you're still not getting it.

FIRST ACTOR: One thing you'll learn about me is that I'm tenacious. When I see something I want, I go for it.

SECOND ACTOR: So does my dog. And I just had him neutered. Look, Walter, you seem like a nice...well, at least you seem like a guy. So why don't you try your luck with one of those zombie-brained bleach blonde bimbos over there? I hear they're into vintage pick-up lines.

FIRST ACTOR: You're not an easy woman to get to know.

SECOND ACTOR: I'm not an easy woman at all. But if you're looking for easy, I will once again refer you to the aforementioned zombie-brained bleach blonde bimbos. Now why don't you be a good boy and go bye-bye before I introduce you to the vet that neutered my dog. *(Pause)* Oh wait, I did it myself with a salad fork.

FIRST ACTOR: Give me a break. I'm trying my best here.

SECOND ACTOR: Yet somehow, still failing miserably. Okay, Walter. Here's the deal... I'm thirsty and PMS-ing, so this is absolutely *not* the right time to try to hit on me. I suggest you go back to chest thumping with Bubba and the boys over in the corner, in order to salvage what little is left of your male pride. Otherwise, I may be tempted to let this half empty bottle of Jim Beam get all cutesy with your facial features.

FIRST ACTOR: *(Rising)* Right. Well, uh... It's been charming.

SECOND ACTOR: For you, maybe. Not for me. You ruined a wonderfully intimate moment I was trying to have with this eighteen year-old Scotch, and now you owe me another. So I suggest you leave some cash on the bar. A ten should do it. A twenty would stop me from telling everyone you have herpes and projectile diarrhea. *(He hesitates. Then drops a $20)* Good choice. You can say bye-bye now. Come on. Say it!

FIRST ACTOR: Uh, bye-bye. *(Exits quickly)*

SECOND ACTOR: I don't get it. *(Sighs)* Why can't I just meet a nice, normal guy... and somehow resist the temptation to shoot him?

146.

FIRST ACTOR: What's for dinner?

SECOND ACTOR: How could you?!

FIRST ACTOR: Hmmmm. That sounds Native American. I was hoping for a bit of French or Greek.

SECOND ACTOR: I'm not talking about dinner. I'm talking about your behavior!

FIRST ACTOR: Well, there again, I was hoping for a bit of French or Greek... Kidding! It was a joke!

SECOND ACTOR: I just got off the phone with my sister.

FIRST ACTOR: Oh, and.... how is she, um, doing?

SECOND ACTOR: She said you tried to kiss her!

FIRST ACTOR: Well, to be perfectly accurate, she tried to kiss me. She had the forward momentum. And I was merely protecting my face with....um...my lips.

SECOND ACTOR: She said you sucked on her tongue!

FIRST ACTOR: Only to avoid choking on it! She had it halfway down my throat, the little vixen...

SECOND ACTOR: How could you?

FIRST ACTOR: Listen, I'm innocent here.

SECOND ACTOR: Innocent? Innocent? Innocent!

FIRST ACTOR: No, that would be more like redundant.

SECOND ACTOR: She's my little sister!

FIRST ACTOR: I know. And I feel wretched about it. But didn't you always want me to get closer to your family? I'm kidding!

147.

FIRST ACTOR: Did you see it?!

SECOND ACTOR: Oh, man. I can't believe it!

FIRST ACTOR: Neither could I! And we were right there! Right in the middle of it!

SECOND ACTOR: We couldn't have planned it better!

FIRST ACTOR: This is something I'm gonna be able to tell my kids one day. Maybe even my grandkids! They'll say, did you hear about that? And I'll say…hear about it? I was there!

SECOND ACTOR: They won't believe you.

FIRST ACTOR: Doesn't matter. I'll know it's true.

SECOND ACTOR: It's hard to believe, man. We were right there!

FIRST ACTOR: Yeah. Right there.

SECOND ACTOR: *(Pause)* You didn't actually see anything, did you?

FIRST ACTOR: No. I was in the bathroom the whole time. How about you?

SECOND ACTOR: Unh-unh. The tall guy with the big hair blocked everything.

FIRST ACTOR: *(Pause)* Doesn't matter, because we were right there!

SECOND ACTOR: Yeah! Right in the middle of it! Let's see if anyone posted it on YouTube yet.

148.

FIRST ACTOR: Hi. Are you…Julie?

SECOND ACTOR: Uh…That depends…

FIRST ACTOR: It's me. Bernie. I mean… "Suave&Sexy94."

SECOND ACTOR: No way. You're Suave&Sexy94?

FIRST ACTOR: In the flesh. We had a coffee date. I'm glad you could make it.

SECOND ACTOR: Wait a minute. According to your Online Dating Profile, you are six-foot-three, athletic and toned, and most comfortable in a tuxedo.

FIRST ACTOR: I might have exaggerated a little. And you really don't expect me to wear a tuxedo to Starbucks, do you?

SECOND ACTOR: You don't look anything like your photos.

FIRST ACTOR: Sure, I do. I just haven't had a chance to post new ones.

SECOND ACTOR: Since when? The Clinton administration? Is that even your real hair?

FIRST ACTOR: Of course, it is. I bought it last week. There's a great toupee shop on Second Avenue.

SECOND ACTOR: Uh-huh. They probably give a discount if you show up in a tux.

FIRST ACTOR: I'm sensing a bit of hostility here. That really hurts my feelings.

SECOND ACTOR: Okay, so the only accurate thing about your dating profile so far is 'sensitive.' What else did you lie about? Friendly and outgoing?

FIRST ACTOR: I have to be. I'm a greeter at Wal-Mart.

SECOND ACTOR: Successful Entrepreneur?

FIRST ACTOR: I sell a little weed on the side.

SECOND ACTOR: Salary: One hundred and fifty thousand plus?

FIRST ACTOR: Well, if you add up the last ten or twelve years…
SECOND ACTOR: Never married?
FIRST ACTOR: That one's true.
SECOND ACTOR: There's a surprise. Well, this has been entertaining, but I think I have to go…
FIRST ACTOR: Where? To your job as a Victoria Secret model and newly appointed Ambassador to Germany?
SECOND ACTOR: Yeah, about that….

149.

FIRST ACTOR: Here I am.
SECOND ACTOR: Wow. You look…
FIRST ACTOR: Incredible? Gorgeous? Incredibly gorgeous?
SECOND ACTOR: D. All of the above.
FIRST ACTOR: Thank you for noticing.
SECOND ACTOR: I'd be a fool not to.
FIRST ACTOR: We both know that being a fool is something you do on a near constant basis. But it was nice that you finally rose to the occasion.
SECOND ACTOR: There was an insult in there, if I'm not mistaken. I give you a compliment and you hand me an insult.
FIRST ACTOR: That's the only way to keep you in line. It's what makes our relationship so exciting, don't you think?
SECOND ACTOR: Yes, I do think. But I didn't realize I was in a relationship with you.
FIRST ACTOR: Like you said…you'd be a fool not to…

150.

FIRST ACTOR: And where do you think you're going?

SECOND ACTOR: To school.

FIRST ACTOR: Not dressed like that, you aren't.

SECOND ACTOR: What did you say?

FIRST ACTOR: You're not going to school in that outfit.

SECOND ACTOR: First off, yes, I am. Secondly, what's wrong with the way I'm dressed?

FIRST ACTOR: It's inappropriate.

SECOND ACTOR: Inappropriate? In what way?

FIRST ACTOR: It sends the wrong signals.

SECOND ACTOR: It's a business suit. And I teach Cross Media Marketing Techniques to graduate students!

FIRST ACTOR: Don't take that tone with me, young lady. As long as you live under my roof, you'll follow my rules!

SECOND ACTOR: Sorry, Dad, but I'm not a little girl anymore. I'm twenty-nine years old, and I've been able to dress myself for quite a few years now. And in case you forgot, this is my house. You moved in after Mom left. So, it's technically it's my roof. My rules.

FIRST ACTOR: Don't give me that attitude. I was the one who had to wipe your butt when you were a baby. You know how many times you spit up on me over the years?

SECOND ACTOR: *(Sighs)* 'Bye, Dad. I have a class to teach.

FIRST ACTOR: You know how many diapers of yours I changed? Do you? Huh?

SECOND ACTOR: Have a good day. I'll see you when I get home.

FIRST ACTOR: I'm talking to you, missy!!

SECOND ACTOR: *(Exiting)* Love you, Dad. Bye!

About The Author

Vin Morreale, Jr. is an award-winning screenwriter, acting teacher, casting director and internationally produced playwright.

Vin was a founding member of the San Francisco Playwrights Center and the Senseless Bickering Comedy Theatre. He has directed hundreds of works for stage, screen and radio across the country.

As president of *Vin Morreale Casting*, along with his nationally known *Burning Up The Stage* acting workshops, he has helped nearly 30,000 actors find work in movies, TV, stage and video.

Vin was awarded the prestigious *Al Smith Writing Fellowship*, and his scripts, stage plays, documentaries, museum exhibits and radio comedy have received hundreds of productions around the world, as well as being translated into Chinese, Italian, Russian and Spanish.

Vin has sold material to network and cable television networks, had feature screenplays optioned and produced, and his work has been seen in more than 15 countries. He was named a top screenwriter by both The International Screenwriters Association and The Blacklist.org.

You can find more of his books at *academyartspress.com*.

And be sure to check out the exciting opportunities at *300monologues.com*.